The Messianic Significance of the Unique Readings in the Large Isaiah Scroll (1QISaᵃ)

The Messianic Significance of the Unique Readings in the Large Isaiah Scroll (1QISaᵃ)

Yeshwanth Bakkavemana

2020

The Messianic Significance of the Unique Readings in the Large Isaiah Scroll (1QISaᵃ)– Published by the Indian Society for Promoting Christian Knowledge (ISPCK), Post Box 1585, Kashmere Gate, Delhi-110006.

ISBN: 978-81-949231-7-6

Laser typeset by

ISPCK, Post Box 1585, 1654, Madarsa Road, Kashmere Gate, Delhi-110006 • *Tel:* 23866323

e-mail: ashish@ispck.org.in • ella@ispck.org.in
website: www.ispck.org.in

Dedication

To my wife Sapana Ghising

רַבּוֹת בָּנוֹת עָשׂוּ חָיִל
וְאַתְּ עָלִית עַל־כֻּלָּנָה :

Proverbs 31:29

Contents

Acknowledgements

I am filled with gratitude towards God for enabling me to study His word. My fascination for the Qumran studies began in one of the Master's courses, which was facilitated by Dr. Eliya Mohol. I am indebted to him as he constructively guided me in the initial stages of my research. It is my honour and privilege to have been supervised by Dr. Paulson Pulikottil, who with his sharp acumen and expertise, guided me in my research. Equally, I am grateful to Dr. Praveen Paul for his guidance and support. Words cannot express the depth my gratitude to my mentor, Rev. Dr. Charles L. Echols who has been my support during my research. Dr. Echols has been my great source of inspiration and encouragement throughout my research and he continues to be so.

My research would not have been successful had it not been for an academic ethos of Union Biblical Seminary. I am grateful to the administration for providing me the resources and other facilities that I could use during my research.

I am deeply indebted to my parents, Mr. Dhananjaya B.V and Mrs. T. Sarah Krupavathi who has sponsored my Masters studies and earnestly prayed for me. At the same time, I would not have seen this day, had it not been for the unconditional support, love, care, and sacrifice of my beloved wife Sapana Ghising, my daughter, Sarah Anjali, and my son, Elijah Sudarsan.

I also want to thank my friends Rev. Vara Joseph Deepak Raj Kumar, Rev. John Jebeseelan Baskaran, Rev. Moses Boosa, Rev. Samuel George Makasare, Ms. Vini Yeptho, Mrs. Akanksha Samuel Makasare and Ms. Sharon V. Awomi, and Dr. N. Subramani for their consistent support and encouragement during the course of my research.

It is my prayer that this work may inspire students of Biblical studies to take up similar researches to fill the gap in our understanding of these amazing Qumran Dead Sea Scrolls.

Foreword

In a sense, teaching is a handshake between the teacher and the student; the former commits to providing knowledge and the latter commits to learning it. A good teacher, though, hopes for more, viz. to learn from the student—especially, at the graduate level, that the student will go on to excel beyond the teacher.

My "handshake" with the author occurred in the fall of 2008. I had completed a PhD at Cambridge a few years earlier and was teaching bachelor and master's students from 2008-2013 at Union Biblical Seminary in Pune, India. I certainly expected to learn from my students—all the more as an expat—and, indeed, the expectation was fulfilled in ways I could not have anticipated. One of my classes was an introduction to the Old Testament. I walked into the classroom, roster in hand, to see the faces of sixty-five young men and women from a multitude of cultures, mostly from the subcontinent. I recall the anxiety of not having a clue how to pronounce over half their names, and, wondering whether some like "Julius Caesar" were someone having fun at my expense. Some three weeks into the course, three students asked to see me after class. When their peers had filed out, they said, "Sir, we don't understand what you're saying." I was taken aback and asked them what technical terms were unclear. "Sir," they replied, "We don't understand your accent." Fortunately, the ancient reverence for the guru still existed. As a "guru," I was accorded much respect and forbearance which I appreciated as I attempted to learn names, speak comprehensibly, and tailor Western material to an Asian audience.

Things were somewhat easier in my second year. One of the names on the roster of Introduction to the Old Testament was Yeshwanth Bakkavemana. He enrolled in further courses with me, all of which had a Hebrew reading component. It became clear that he was sincere, motivated, and a hard worker, and our relationship began. In my judgment the "birth" of a scholar occurs on the embarkation of the first thesis. The transition from being handed a syllabus to figuring out your own is exciting and daunting. My greatest joy as a professor is to be "midwife" in a student's transition from taught classes to independent research. As Yeshwanth navigated the transition, I recognized further qualities which I knew would take him where he is today. I discovered that he is also resilient. As he encountered the inevitable twists and turns in the road to a thesis, he rebounded from distress and uncertainty and pushed on to clarity and resolution. The delight of being a thesis supervisor often extends beyond books. From the initial months of encouragement, the student begins to see the supervisor as a confidant and a mentor. It was a pleasure and a sacred honor to serve in that capacity for Yeshwanth as he thought through challenges during his term as a student body present and matters such as vocational clarity, family, friendships, and his walk with the Lord.

After I returned to the U.S. in 2013, Yeshwanth completed his bachelor's degree and served as Academic Dean at a Nepal Ebenezer Bible College from 2013-2015. However, we kept in touch, and the occasional research that he asked me to proof evinced continuing scholarly growth and competence in conducting independent research.

A master's degree (2016-2018) provided further maturation as a scholar. Drawing on his bachelor's study of Hebrew and textual criticism, he turned to the Dead Sea Scrolls, focusing on the Great Isaiah Scroll (1QIsaa) for his thesis. Providentially, he was supervised by Paulson Pulikottil, an expert in the Scrolls and my former and much-appreciated colleague. The present volume is a revision of the thesis, which was approved in 2018. The monograph applies several methodologies to variant readings in 1QIsaa to unearth and elucidate any messianic significance in the scroll.

I hope that the handshake that began in 2008 has been as fruitful to Yeshwanth as it has been to me. It helped me to hone pedagogical skills, grow in competence in Hebrew and in supervising, and expand my field of knowledge. Perhaps more importantly, it has afforded me joy—from supervisions, to matters of the heart, to seeing my former student become a colleague and friend.

The Rev. Charles L. Echols, Ph.D.

Preface

This work is a revised version of my Master of Theology thesis in the department of Biblical Studies, Old Testament, from the Senate of Serampore College (University). This research is an attempt to find out whether the unique readings of the Large Isaiah Scroll (1QIsaa) have any messianic significance. These Unique readings are the variants which are not attested by any witness but have some ideological affinities with other biblical and Qumran literature. While exploring the messianic significance of the Unique readings, this research seeks to find out the theological milieu of the Scroll. In order to establish the above hypothesis, textual criticism is employed. The aim of the textual criticism in the research is not to adjudicate the text that is closer to the *Urtext* but to find scribal intentions behind the unique readings. Therefore, along with textual criticism, the research employs syntactical and grammatical analysis to find out distinct messianic ideas behind the unique readings. Furthermore, harmonization method is employed to find out ideological milieu of the Scroll.

The research analyzed the select unique readings from Paulson Pulikottil's book *Transmission of Biblical Texts in Qumran The Case of the Large Isaiah Scroll 1QIsaa*. The research found out seven distinct messianic ideas reflected by the select unique readings.

These messianic ideas were analyzed using harmonization method to find out ideological affinities with other biblical and Qumran literature. Besides finding out the messianic ideas behind the select unique readings resonated with Yaḥad messianic sensibilities in general, it was found out that the Scroll is more inclined to 1QS Messianism. Therefore, the messianic milieu of the Scroll may be Yaḥad but more inclined to 1QS.

he implications of this research extends to textual, theological, and sociological studies in OT and Qumran studies. The method employed would be beneficial to similar studies so that the "conceptual gaps" between OT and NT may be filled. Such an endeavor would call for a different way of using textual criticism as this research employed. In that textual criticism can be used to find out scribal intentions behind the variants. This helps us to have a comprehensive understanding of the theological and ideological development during the Second Temple Period.

Yeshwanth Bakkavemana
Union Biblical Seminary,
9th Oct 2020

Abbreviations

[ ]	Brackets indicate reconstructed texts or gaps
√	Root of
AB	Anchor Bible
ABRL	Anchor Bible Reference Library
Acc	Accusative
Act	Active
BA	Biblical Archaeology
BASOR	Bulletin of the American Schools of Oriental Research
BETS	Bulletin for Evangelical Theological Society
BHS	Biblical Hebraica Stuttgartensia
Bib	Biblica
CBQ	Catholic Biblical Quarterly
CBQMS	Catholic Biblical Quarterly Monograph Series
CC	Continental Commentaries

Com	Common
Conj	Conjunction
DCH	Dictionary of Classical Hebrew
Deut	Deuteronomy
DJD	Discoveries in the Judean Desert
DSD	Dead Sea Discoveries
et al.	*et alii,* Others
F	Feminine
GKC	*Gesenius' Hebrew Grammar*
Hiph	Hiphil Stem
HTR	Harvard Theological Review
HUCA	Hebrew Union College Annual
ICC	International Critical Commentary
Impf	Imperfect
Inf	Infinitive
JBL	Journal of Biblical Literature
JBQ	Jewish Biblical Quarterly
JJS	Journal for Jewish Studies
JSOT	Journal for the Study of the Old Testament
JSOTSup	Journal for the Study of the Old Testament: Supplement Series
JSPSup	Journal for the Study of the Pseudepigrapha: Supplement Series
JTS	Journal for Theological Studies
LSTS	Library of the Second Temple Period
LXX	Septuagint

Matt	Gospel according to Matthew
MSS	Manuscripts
MT	Masoretic Text
NCB	New Century Bible
NT	New Testament
OEBI	The Oxford Encyclopedia of Biblical Interpretation
OT	Old Testament
OTL	The Old Testament Library
Pass	Passive
Per	Personal
Pft	Perfect
Pr	Press
Pron	Pronoun
Ps	Pronominal suffix
Ptcpl	Participle
Qal	Qal Stem
QSP	Qumran Scribal Practice
RB	Revue Biblique
RevQ	Revue de Qumran
S	singular
Sam. Pent	Samaritan Pentateuch
STDJ	Studies on the Texts of the Desert of Judah
Tg	Targum
TSAJ	Text and Studies in Ancient Judaism

VT	Vestus Testamentum
W/C	Waw-Consecutive
WBC	Word Biblical Commentary
WMANT	*Wissenschaftliche Monographien Zum Alten und Neuen Testament*

Dead Sea Scrolls

1QH	Hodayot document from Qumran Cave 1
1QISa[a]	The Large Isaiah Scroll from Qumran Cave 1
1QISa[b]	Isaiah[b]
1QM	Milḥamah or War Scroll from Qumran Cave 1
1QpHab	Pesher Habakkuk from Qumran Cave 1
1QS	*Serek Hayaḥad or* Rule of the Community from Qumran Cave 1
CD	Cairo Genizah Copy of the Damascus Document
1QS[a] (1Q28a)	Rule of Congregation (Appendix a to 1QS) from Qumran Cave 1
1QS[b] (1Q28b)	Rule of Blessings (Appendix b to 1QS) from Qumran Cave 1
4QSam[a] (4Q51)	Samuel[a]
apocrDan ar (4Q246)	Aramaic Apocalypse
4QFlor (4Q174)	Florilegium, also Midrash on Eschatology[a]
4QPIsa[a] (4Q161)	Pesher Isaiah[a]

4QT (4Q175)	Testimonia
War Scroll (4Q285)	Sefer-ha-Milḥamah (*Olim* Serekh ha-Milḥamah)
4Q521	Messianic Apocalypse
4QAaron A (4Q541)	apocrLevi[b?] ar (*Olim* AhA= TLevi[h? ar])
11QMelch (11Q13)	Melchizedek
11QT[a-b] (11Q 19-20)	Temple Scroll[a-b]

Chapter - 1

Introduction

This book is an exploration, whether the unique readings of the Large Isaiah Scroll (1QIsa^a)[1] has messianic significance. It also attempts to locate the milieu of the Scroll's theological inclination. The variations between the Scroll and the *Masoretic* text (MT) of Isaiah may be due to scribal modifications. These modifications may be intentional or unintentional. Keeping this hypothesis in mind, first this book will investigate the unique readings of the Scroll for messianic significance. Secondly, it will attempt to locate the messianic milieu of the Scroll.

All the variant readings of the Scroll may not be due to scribal errors. There may be certain variants which reflect intentional changes made by the scribe of the Scroll. These intentional changes may indicate an exegetical concern of the scribe in the transmission of the text.[2] Emanuel Tov

---

[1] Here after the Scroll.

[2] Patrick William Skehan, "The Qumran Manuscripts and the Textual Criticism," in *Qumran and the History of the Biblical Text* (ed. Frank Moore Cross and Shemaryahu Talmon; Cambridge, Massachusetts: Harvard University Press, 1978), 215.

observes that these modifications made by the scribe are due to "exegetical, theological, and contextual" concerns of the scribe.[3] In Isa. 45:7, for example, MT reads as עשׂה שׁלום ובורא רע which is translated as "I make *peace* and I create evil."[4] The Scroll replaces the word שׁלום with the word טוב—עשׂה טוב ובורא רע which is translated as "I make *good* and I create evil." This intentional change by the scribe of the Scroll reflects the Scribe's dualistic framework in which both good and bad are created by YHWH.[5] MT, however, seeks to overcome this dualism. Hence there is an interpretative difference between the Scroll and the MT.

However, intentional changes by the scribe may not be sufficient for us to understand the unique contribution of the Scroll. Paulson Pulikottil suggests that the Scroll's disagreement with MT may not be sufficient for us to understand the unique contribution of the scribe.[6] The Scroll's variations might have been attested in the LXX. This suggests that both the Scroll and LXX might have used a source which may be common to both. In Isa 1:13, for instance, the Scroll adds אצבעותיכם בעאוןat the end of the verse, which means "your fingers with iniquity". This is a unique reading which is not attested by any other witnesses. John D. W. Watts

---

[3] Emanuel Tov, *Textual Criticism of the Hebrew Bible* (3d ed.; Minneapolis: Fortress Press, 2012), 240.

[4] Unless and otherwise indicated all the Hebrew translations are the writer's.

[5] Emanuel Tov, *Hebrew Bible, Greek Bible and Qumran: Collected Essays* (TSAJ 121; Tübingen: Mohr Siebeck, 2008), 7–8.

[6] Paulson Pulikottil, *Transmission of Biblical Texts in Qumran The Case of the Large Isaiah Scroll 1QISaa* (JSPSup 34; England: Sheffield Academic Press, 2001), 38.

suggests that the Scroll is making a metrical improvement.[7] Pulikottil is suggestive of a textual harmonization by which the scribe is conceptually harmonizing this verse in the light of Isa 59:3 in which both hands and fingers are mentioned.[8] This book makes use of the select unique readings identified by Pulikottil. These unique readings will be analyzed to find out whether they reflect any significant messianic ideas. The research, consequently, attempts to find out whether these messianic ideas resonate with Yaḥad messianic sensibilities. In doing so, the messianic milieu of the Scroll may be located.

Firstly, the purpose of the book is to investigate the select unique readings of the Scroll to see whether the unique readings reflect any distinct messianic understanding of the Scroll. Secondly, the research attempts to find whether the unique readings resonate with other Qumran literature *viz.*, the Yaḥad documents. The study, conversely, throws light on the scribal activity that played a vital role in the transmission of the text. Thirdly, this book will be resourceful to researchers as it identifies not only text-critical issues related to the variants, but also problems in interpretation of the passages in which these variants arise.

Scope and Limitations of the book

The scope of this book can be extended to other themes in the book of Isaiah such as creation, election, covenant, and worship. An examination of the variants in these thematic

---

[7] John D. W. Watts, *Isaiah 1-33* (WBC 24; Waco, TX: Word Books, Publisher, 1985), 14.

[8] Pulikottil, *Transmission of Biblical Texts*, 206.

passages in the book of Isaiah will help us to understand theological development in the Second Temple Period of which the Scroll represents one facet of such development. The book is limited to analyze the select unique readings which may exhibit significant changes which reflect messianic sensibilities. Keeping this in mind, the book will examine the unique readings in Isa 1, 2, 4, 7, 9, 10, 11, 26, 40, 42, 49, 50, 52-53, 61, and 62. Furthermore, a detailed study of non-biblical scrolls may also help us to understand the scribal activity within the biblical scrolls. However, attention is limited to readings from non-biblical texts found at Qumran for illustrative purposes.

Definitions

The Large Isaiah Scroll (1QIsa^a*)*

The Large Isaiah Scroll refers to the Isaiah scroll found in Cave 1 at Qumran which, again, will be referred as "the Scroll" in the book. The Scroll is significant because it preserves virtually all sixty-six chapters of the book of Isaiah in 54 columns except for few gaps caused by leather damage at the bottom. The measurement of the scroll is 734 x 26.2 cms. The initial research on the Large Isaiah Scroll has been done by Millar Burrows.[9] Following his initial observations, different studies have been published in varied aspects such as the Scroll's scribal activity, orthography, paleography, and variant

---

[9] Millar Burrows, "The Newly Discovered Jerusalem Scrolls II The Contents and Significance of the Manuscripts," *BA* 11.3 (1948): 57–61; Burrows, "Orthography, Morphology, and Syntax of the St Mark's Isaiah Manuscript," *JBL* 68 (1949): 195-211.

readings. The text of this Scroll generally agrees with the MT of the book of Isaiah, but it does, as mentioned earlier, reflect deviations which have interested many scholars.

Masoretic Text (MT)

The Masoretic Text is the eponymous Hebrew text of the Old Testament preserved and standardized by Jews in the final centuries of the first millennium.[10] This will be indicated by the symbol MT. These Jewish scholars existed from 500 to 950 A.D. They gave the final form to OT. After the destruction of the temple in 70 A. D, Jews were scattered. This gave an impetus to standardize the text by introducing punctuation and use of vowels for correct pronunciation and standardized consonantal text.

Scribal Variant

This study understands that scribal variants are not always due to scribal mistakes. The scribal mistakes may be due to minuses, pluses, and interchanges.[11] However, the deviations may be considered as errors if the variants do not fit into logical, grammatical and linguistic context of the text.[12]

Unique Readings

Unique readings, in this book are understood as the variants which are not attested by other witnesses but have some

---

[10] Ernst Würthwein, *The Text of the Old Testament An Introduction to the Biblica Heraica* (2d ed.; trans, Erroll F. Rhodes; Grand Rapids, MI: William B. Eerdmans Publishing Company, 1995), 10.

[11] Tov, *Textual Criticism of the Hebrew Bible*, 221–33.

[12] Pulikottil, *Transmission of Biblical Texts*, 23–24.

ideological affinities with other biblical and Qumran literature. Further explanation to identify the unique readings is given in the third chapter.

Conclusion

In the next chapter an analysis of the select unique readings will be done by using textual criticism. Along with textual criticism, syntactical and grammatical analysis will be done to find the distinct messianic ideas of the Scroll. This chapter is followed by an analysis of these ideas by using harmonization method which is a part of textual criticism. The aim of this chapter is to find textual, contextual, and conceptual affinities with other biblical and Qumran literature. This helps to locate

Chapter 2

Messianic Significance of the Unique Readings in the Scroll

The select unique readings in the Scroll may reflect distinct messianic ideas of the Scroll. Keeping this hypothesis in mind, this chapter first defines unique readings. Secondly, these unique readings will be analyzed for messianic significance by using text-critical and syntactical-grammatical analysis as mentioned in the methodology. Thirdly, distinct messianic ideas of the Scroll will be identified.

Unique readings

The attempt to understand the unique contribution of the Scroll cannot completely rely on the Scroll's deviation from the MT alone. The reason that the variations of the scroll may have been attested elsewhere. Hence, that particular reading or variant may not be considered unique to the scroll. Pulikottil rightly points out that to understand the contribution of the scribe; it is not enough to consider the Scroll's deviation from

MT alone.[1] Keeping this in mind, unique readings in this book are defined as "the readings of the scroll which disagree with BHS and are not attested in other witnesses or where the witnesses are uncertain." Pulikottil has already identified unique readings in his book and proposed a criterion to identify the same. The criterion is 1) the reading of the Scroll is considered unique if it disagrees with LXX; 2) the reading of the Scroll is unique of the reading does not agree with MT and LXX is not uncertain; 3) the reading of the Scroll is unique if there is uncertainty whether Scroll deviated from LXX or *vice versa* and the Scroll's reading is not attested any other witness; and 4) the reading of the Scroll is unique if the readings agree with minor witnesses against MT.[2]

For example, the Scroll's reading in Isa 1:8 reads וכמלונה for כִּמְלוּנָה in MT is attested in LXX, Syriac, Peshita, and Latin Vulgate. Hence this is not considered as Unique reading in the scroll. This book will make use of Pulikottil's unique readings to analyze them whether there are any distinct messianic ideas reflected by the Scroll.

The book will also analyze the unique readings of the Scroll to find out whether the unique readings reflect any messianic significance. Then the unique readings in Isa 1, 2, 4, 7, 9, 10, 11, 26, 40, 42, 49, 50, 52:13-53, 61, and 62 will be discussed.

---

[1] Pulikottil, *Transmission of Biblical Texts*, 38.

[2] Pulikottil, *Transmission of Biblical Texts*, 39–40.

Analysis of the Unique Readings for Messianic Significance

Isaiah 1

Isaiah 1:24

In Isaiah 1, only one unique reading has messianic significance.

MT

אֶנָּחֵם מִצָּרַי וְאִנָּקְמָה מֵאוֹיְבָי׃

I will pour out my wrath on my enemies and avenge myself on my foes

Scroll

אנחם מצריו ואנקם מאובו

I will pour out my wrath on *his* enemies and avenge myself on *his* foes

The issue here is the change in pronominal suffixes. MT renders first common pronominal suffix whereas the Scroll renders third masculine pronominal suffix. E. Y. Kutscher notes this variant as scribal error as he finds that here the letters are misplaced and suspended.[3] However, John V. Chamberlain understands this as messianic variant. He notes that the antecedent of מצריו and מאובו (his enemies and his foes) is צֶדֶק (Righteous) which corresponds to the Teacher of Righteousness in the Qumran literature.[4] Van der

---

[3] Edward Yechezkel Kutscher, *The Language and Linguistic Background of the Isaiah Scroll 1 QIsaa* (Leiden: Brill, 1974), 531.

[4] Chamberlain, "Functions of God as Messianic Titles in the Complete Qumran Isaiah Scroll," 370–72.

Kooij basing on Chamberlain's suggestion understands and personifies צדק. In that צדק is the Teacher of Righteousness whose enemy is the wicked priests.[5] However, Pulikottil does not agree with Kooij and Chamberlain. He points out that the personification of צדק is a false assumption and nowhere in the Qumran is texts צדק mentioned as the Teacher of Righteousness.[6] He further notes that the third person masculine pronoun can also be used to indicate inanimate things.[7] However, interpretative intentions cannot be ruled out. Pulikottil points to this aspect in Isa 9:6 where the Scroll reads third masculine singular pronominal suffix for a second feminine pronominal suffix.[8] Therefore, based on the Scroll's reading, there is an interpretative difference which indicates the Scroll's distinct messianic ideology. MT interprets the text as "the kind of activity which hitherto had been undertaken on behalf of his people against their enemies is now turned back against them."[9] On the other hand, Scroll interprets the text as God's vengeance on behalf of Messiah against his enemies. In other words, the distinct messianic idea of the Scroll is warrior messiah who would act on his behalf and fight his enemies, in this case, within Israel.[10]

---

[5] Arie van der Kooij, *Die Alten Textzeugen Des Jesajabuches* (Fribourg, Switzerland: Universitätsverlag; Vandenhoeck & Ruprecht, 1981) as cited by Pulikottil, *Transmission of Biblical Texts, 26.*

[6] Pulikottil, *Transmission of Biblical Texts, 27.*

[7] Pulikottil, *Transmission of Biblical Texts, 27.*

[8] Pulikottil, *Transmission of Biblical Texts, 114.*

[9] Williamson, *Isaiah 1-5,* 143.

[10] Chamberlain, "Functions of God as Messianic Titles in the Complete Qumran Isaiah Scroll," 370–71.

Isaiah 2

Isaiah 2:3

Isaiah 2:3 is a unique reading that reflects some messianic significance.

MT

וְהָלְכוּ עַמִּים רַבִּים וְאָמְרוּ לְכוּ וְנַעֲלֶה אֶל־הַר־יְהוָה אֶל־בֵּית אֱלֹהֵי יַעֲקֹב

וְיֹרֵנוּ מִדְּרָכָיו וְנֵלְכָה בְּאֹרְחֹתָיו כִּי מִצִּיּוֹן תֵּצֵא תוֹרָה וּדְבַר־יְהוָה מִירוּשָׁלָםִ:

Many people shall come and say, "let us go! Let us go up to the mountain of the LORD, to the house of God of Jacob, that he may teach us his way, so that we may walk in his paths, For out of Zion shall come forth Torah, and the word of the LORD from Jerusalem."

Scroll

והלכו עמים ואמרו לכו ונעלה אל בית אלוהי יעקוב

וירונו מדרציו ונלכה בארחותיו כי מציון תצא תורה ודבר יהוה מירושלם

Many people shall come and say, "Let us go! And go to the house of God of Jacob, that *they* may teach us his ways, so that we may walk in his paths. For out or Zion shall come forth Torah, and the word of the LORD from Jerusalem."

There are two issues here. First one is omission of the phrase אל־הר־יהוה (the mountain of the LORD) in the Scroll. Second one is plural form of the verb ירה (to teach). Williamson considers the former i.e., the omission of "the mountain of the LORD" as *parablepsis* and the later a metathesis.[11] However, a close examination proves that this

---

[11] Williamson, *Isaiah 1-5*, 170.

is an intentional change made by the scribe of the scroll. For example, Pulikottil argues that since the omission of the phrase "the mountain of the LORD" does not create any syntactical difficulty, this cannot be considered as scribal error. Furthermore, the verb וירונו is a plural which is syntactically correct. Conversely, the change has been made in the light of אחרית ימים (end of days) in v.2. In that the Scroll agrees with MT and the versions regarding the importance of the mount Zion. However, the Scroll deviates from MT regarding Jerusalem as the center of religion where Law is taught. In the Scroll the center of religion is בית אלוהי יעקוב (the house of God of Jacob). In MT, Torah is taught by the LORD whereas in the Scroll it is "they." The messianic significance is in the reference to the Torah and also those who are responsible to teach. The responsibility to teach is one of the functions of Messiah/s at the end of days in the Qumran scrolls[12] which we will discuss in the following chapter.

Isaiah 4

Isaiah 4:2

In the fourth chapter, verse 2 is a unique reading which reflects messianic sensibility.

MT

בַּיּוֹם הַהוּא יִהְיֶה צֶמַח יְהוָה

לִצְבִי וּלְכָבוֹד וּפְרִי הָאָרֶץ לְגָאוֹן וּלְתִפְאֶרֶת לִפְלֵיטַת יִשְׂרָאֵל:

---

[12] John J. Collins, *The Scepter and the Star Messianism in the Light of the Dead Sea Scrolls* (2d ed.; Grand Rapids, MI: Eerdmans, 2010), 110.

On that day the branch of the LORD shall be beautiful and glorious, and the fruit of the land shall be pride and glory of the survivors of Israel.

Scroll

ביום ההוא יהיה צמח יהוה לצבי ולצבי ולכבווד ופרי

הארץ לגאון ולתפארת לפליטת ישראל ויהודה

On that day the branch of the LORD shall be beautiful and glorious, and the fruit of the land shall be pride and glory of the survivors of Israel *and Judah.*

The issue is addition of ויהודה (and Judah) which is an explicatory addition. However, Rosenbloom considers this to be a case of careless scribal error.[13] Williamson notes that the expression ישראל ויהודה (Israel and Judah) is a unique expression which appears only here in this verse.[14] However, the scribe of the Scroll might have added "Judah" under the influence of similar phrases that we find in Isa 5:7 and 37:31.[15] On the other hand, Daniel D. Stuhlman notes that the addition may refer to the divided kingdoms of Israel and Judah or to show differences between the same or simply a poetic parallelism.[16] Moreover in Jer 31: 27 and Ezek 4:4-6 there is a reference to Israel and Judah. Watts notes that in Isaiah the fate of Israel from Judah consciously separated.

---

[13] Rosenbloom, *The Dead Sea Isaiah Scroll*, 10.

[14] Williamson, *Isaiah 1-5*, 301.

[15] Arie Rubinstein, "The Theological Aspect of Some Variant Readings in the Isaiah Scroll," *JJS* 6.4 (1955): 188.

[16] Daniel D Stuhlman, "A Variant Text from the Isaiah Scroll," *JBQ* 25.3 (1997): 179.

So, syntactically and grammatically the addition does not pose any textual difficulty. Furthermore, in connection with צמח (branch), the fate of Judah is also included with that of Israel.[17] In addition to this, the messianic significance of this verse lies in connection with צמח יהוה (branch of the LORD). Hans Wildberger points out that this text in Targum translates this as משיחא דיהוה (the Messiah of Yahweh) which indicates that Targum understood צמח יהוה as messianic title.[18] Watts, similarly notes that the word צמח carries royal messianic significance.[19] Paul Swarup observes that this word carries messianic significance especially in relation Qumran community's self understanding as "the 'root of the planting,' a part of post-exilic remnant, a community which has been raised by God to bring his promises to the prophets to fruition."[20] Keeping this in mind, the interpretative difference between MT and the Scroll is that MT seems to use ישראל as *double entendre*.[21] On the other hand, the Scroll makes it very explicit by adding Judah thus importing a new meaning to the text. This new meaning can be identified in relation to

---

[17] Watts, *Isaiah 1-33*, 48.

[18] Hans Wildberger, *Isaiah 1-12 A Commentary* (CC 24; trans. Thomas Trapp; Minneapolis: Augsburg Fortress, 1991), 165.

[19] Watts, *Isaiah 1-33*, 48.

[20] Paul Swarup, *The Self-Understanding of the Dead Sea Scrolls Community: An Eternal Planting, a House of Holiness* (LSTS 59; London: T&T Clark, 2006), 83.

[21] Double entendre is otherwise called as "Polysemantic pun" in which a word can have two or more meanings. The efficacy of this usage is in its witt that attracts the attention of the hearers, see, Wilfred G. E. Watson, *Classical Hebrew Poetry A Guide to Its Techniques* (JSOTSup 26; Sheffield: JSOT Pr, 1986), 241.

the phrase צמח יהוה. In that צמח carries messianic idea that reflects individually as a title for the Davidic messiah and also to the community as the "root of the planting." Therefore, this unique reading does carry messianic significance.

Isaiah 7

Isaiah 7:14

In Isaiah 7, one unique reading is identified. The reading is not attested in any other witnesses.

MT

וְקָרָאת שְׁמוֹ עִמָּנוּ אֵל׃

And she called his name Immanuel.

Scroll

וקרא שמו עממנו אל

And He called his name Immanuel.

The issue here is the change in gender of the subject. Who named Immanuel? Is it God or the woman? There are two possibilities to this reading. First, Joseph R. Rosenbloom points out that the Scroll agrees with LXX, though differently. LXX renders καλέσεις (you shall name) which is a second person masculine verb which makes the prophet the subject of שמו.[22] Secondly, if שמו is considered as the subject then קרא has to be pointed as *pual* וְקֹרָא (and his name shall be

---

[22] Rosenbloom, *The Dead Sea Isaiah Scroll*, 15.

called).[23] However, the Scroll reads the verb as וְקָרָא (Conj + Qal Pft third masculine singular)—"and he called." This indicates that the Scroll intends God to be the subject of קרא.[24] Similarly, R. E. Clements notes that the variants does not resolve the issue and therefore, the Scroll reading may be accepted as it is God who gives assurances and names.[25] It is his prerogative. Moreover, John D. W. Watts notes that the whole passage has messianic significance. He pointed out the change of addressee in Isa 7:13 from Ahaz to בית דויד (house of David).[26] Joseph Blenkinsopp points out that the phrase בית דויד in the scroll has royal messianic significance.[27] In addition to this, R. E. Brown notes that the naming the child is the base for the paternity.[28] In that a man names his child to acknowledge him/her to be his own. The same phenomenon is reflected in the Scroll where God names the Messianic child. This is legitimization of Messiah as the Son of God. Therefore, at Isa 7:14, the Scroll seems to amplify or emphasize YHWH's authority in giving a messianic son and christening him who would bring peace and order. In this way the Scroll's interpretation deviates from *MT*. In that Isa 7:14 has messianic significance.

---

[23] The verb is read as 3fs which is translated as "she named him," see, GKC § 72g.

[24] Pulikottil, *Transmission of Biblical Texts*, 87.

[25] R. E. Clements, *Isaiah 1-39* (NCB; Grand Rapids, MI: Wm. B. Eerdmans Publishing, 1980), 86.

[26] Watts, *Isaiah 1-33*, 24:95.

[27] Blenkinsopp, *Isaiah 1-39*, 246.

[28] Raymond Edward Brown, *The Birth of the Messiah: A Commentary on the Infancy Narratives in the Gospels of Matthew and Luke* (ABRL; NY: Doubleday; Geoffrey Chapman, 1993), 139.

Isaiah 9

In chapter 9, there are two unique readings that carry messianic significance.

Isaiah 9:5

The Scroll reads as השלום for שלום in MT. This reading indicates explicative interest of the Scroll that is undergirded by the specific understanding of the שלום. The addition of the article may also indicate that the word is a title.[29] John J. Collins relates 9:5 with the thanksgiving hymn in the *Hodayot* document 1QH 3.[30] Collins finds lot of allusions especially regarding the birth imagery. According to him, birth imagery is often connected to the advent of Messiah.[31] Furthermore, Watts points out that the Targum renders as מפלי עיעא אלהא גינירא קיים עלמיא משיחא דשלמא יסגי עלנא ביומוהו which is translated as "Wonderful counselor, mighty God who live forever, the Messiah in whom the days peace will be great over us."[32] Therefore, this particular unique reading has messianic significance. The interpretative difference is that MT does not understand the word סולש as a title, but the Scroll does. The distinct messianic idea of this variant has to do with the concept of peace which has messianic connotations in the Qumran literature.

---

[29] Pulikottil, *Transmission of Biblical Texts*, 91.

[30] Collins, *The Scepter and the Star*, 75–76.

[31] Collins, *The Scepter and the Star*, 76.

[32] Watts, *Isaiah 1-33*, 131.

Isaiah 9:6

MT

לְמַרְבֵּה הַמִּשְׂרָה וּלְשָׁלוֹם אֵין־קֵץ עַל־כִּסֵּא דָוִד וְעַל־מַמְלַכְתּוֹ לְהָכִין אֹתָהּ
וּלְסַעֲדָהּ בְּמִשְׁפָּט וּבִצְדָקָה מֵעַתָּה וְעַד־עוֹלָם קִנְאַת יְהוָה צְבָאוֹת תַּעֲשֶׂה־זֹּאת: ס

Abundant authority and peace without end, for the throne
of David, and upon his kingdom. To establish and uphold
her with justice and righteousness from now and forevermore.
The Zeal of the LORD of Hosts will do this.

Scroll

למרבה המשרה ולשלום אין קץ על כסה דויד ועל ממלכתו להכין אותו ולסעדו
במשפט ובצדקה מעתה ועד עולם קנאת יהוה צבאות תעשה זאת

Abundant authority and peace without end, for the throne of
David and upon his kingdom. To establish and uphold *him*
with justice and righteousness from now and forevermore.
The Zeal of the LORD of Hosts will do this.

The issue is regarding changes in pronominal suffix
in the phrase הכין אותו ולסעדו. MT has third feminine
singular pronominal suffix whereas the Scroll reads it as third
masculine singular pronominal suffix. LXX agrees with MT as
it reads κατορθῶσαι αυτὴν (Verb+Inf+Aorist+act+Per pron
acc f s—"to support her") and the antecedent of αυτὴν is a
feminine noun βασιλεία (kingdom). However, in the light of
v. 5, the Scroll reads the object of the verbs (כון "to establish"
and סעד "to uphold") as the ילד (child) in which it refers to
Messianic child. Clearly the Scroll's focus is on Messianic child
than the Davidic kingdom. Hence there exists interpretative

difference. Pulikottil rightly notes that this unique reading has interpretative effect.[33] In that MT understands the verse as the establishment of Davidic kingdom whereas the Scroll reads as the establishment of the kingdom of Messianic child. This idea of God begetting, and naming Messiah is very much prevalent Ancient West Asian culture.[34] Furthermore, this verse has conceptual allusions of "Son of God" in Ps. 2:7-8 and 2 Sam 7:14. Therefore, this verse has messianic significance. The distinct messianic idea of the Scroll has to do with Messianic child/ Son of God.

Isaiah 10

The unique reading at Isa 10:24 reflect messianic significance.

Isaiah 10:24

MT

לָכֵן כֹּה־אָמַר אֲדֹנָי יְהוִה צְבָאוֹת אַל־תִּירָא עַמִּי יֹשֵׁב צִיּוֹן מֵאַשּׁוּר

בַּשֵּׁבֶט יַכֶּכָּה וּמַטֵּהוּ יִשָּׂא־עָלֶיךָ בְּדֶרֶךְ מִצְרָיִם׃

Therefore thus says the Lord God of Hosts, "O my people who live in Zion, do not be afraid on account of Assyria when they beat you with a rod and lift up their staff against you as the Egyptians.

---

[33] Pulikottil, *Transmission of Biblical Texts*, 114.

[34] Wildberger, *Isaiah 1-12*, 408.

Scroll

לכן כוה אמר אדוני יהוה צבאות אל תידא אמי יושב ציון מאשור

משבט יככה ומטו ישא עליך בדרך מצרים

Therefore thus says the Lord God of Hosts, "O my people, who live in Zion, do not be afraid on account of Assyria when they beat you *on account of the rod* and lift up their staff against you as the Egyptians.

The issue here is regarding the objects of the verb ירא (to fear). In MT שבט is the dependent on אשור (Assyria). However, in the Scroll both שבט and אשור are dependent on the verb ירא. In v. 26 YHWH's מטה (rod) will overcome waters. In other words, the rod of YHWH will overcome the rod of Assyria. It is to be noted that the word שבט is not used in v.26 but rather the word מטה is used. There is a parallelism between v. 24 and v. 26. In that שבט and מטה are synonymously used.[35] This parallelism emphasizes the contrast between the rod of Assyria and the rod of YHWH. Furthermore, the word שבט has messianic significance. For example, in Num 24:17, the word comes as a title "שבט מישראל" that has messianic meaning. Furthermore, this word is well attested in Qumran literature and carries messianic significance. Therefore, this unique reading has messianic importance. The interpretative difference is that MT does not read this verse with messianic significance whereas the Scroll does. In that the Scroll attempts make explicit contrast between the rod of Assyria and the rod of YHWH.

---

[35] David J. A. Clines, "מַטֶּה," *DCH* V: 237.

The distinct messianic idea has to do with the שבט —the scepter in a war context. So, a picture of "warrior messiah" can be observed which is attested in the Qumran literature.

Isaiah 11

Three unique readings have been identified with messianic significance in this passage.

Isaiah 11:1

Pulikottil does not mention this as unique reading in his work. However, the variant here is not attested elsewhere.

MT

וְיָצָא חֹטֶר מִגֶּזַע יִשָׁי וְנֵצֶר מִשָּׁרָשָׁיו יִפְרֶה׃

A Shoot will come out from the stump of Jesse, and a branch shall come out of his roots.

The issue here is that the Scroll omits the second line i.e., ונצר משרשיו יפרה (and a branch shall come out of his roots). Moreover, this cannot be regarded as scribal error as the omission does not issue any syntactical difficulty. Pulikottil rightly assumes that unless the variant does not create grammatical or linguistic difficulty or creates inconsistency in the logical meaning of the verse, the reading is not considered as error.[36] Jasper Hoegenhaven similarly argues in the case of the Scroll that the scribe of the Scroll is extremely meticulous in copying the text.[37] Keeping this in mind, the Scroll seems

---

[36] Pulikottil, *Transmission of Biblical Texts*, 24.

[37] Hoegenhaven, "The First Isaiah Scroll from Qumran (1QIsa) and the Massoretic Text," 25.

to avoid an interpretation that "another branch" will come out from the roots. This reading resonates a sectarian ideology as well. Furthermore, the concept of "the shoot of Jesse" is well attested in the Bible and other Qumran literature. For example, in Jer 33:15 textual allusions to the above verse can be found. The key word צמח appears here as well which is considered as synonym to חטר (branch). Moreover, the branch imagery is well attested in AWA royal motifs.[38] Therefore, this unique reading reflects a distinct messianic idea of the Scroll in which צמח/חטר has messianic connotations which are also attested in the Qumran literature.

Isaiah 11:4

MT

וְשָׁפַט בְּצֶדֶק דַּלִּים וְהוֹכִיחַ בְּמִישׁוֹר לְעַנְוֵי־אָרֶץ וְהִכָּה־אֶרֶץ

בְּשֵׁבֶט פִּיו וּבְרוּחַ שְׂפָתָיו יָמִית רָשָׁע׃

And He shall judge the poor with righteousness and He shall decide with equity for poor of the land, and he shall strike the land with the rod of his mouth and with the breath of his lips he shall kill the wicked.

Scroll

ושפט בצדק דלים והוכיח במישור לענוי הארץ והכה

הארץ בשבט קיו וברוח שפתיו ימית רשע

---

[38] Collins, *The Scepter and the Star29*; Joseph A Fitzmyer, *The Dead Sea Scrolls and the Christian Origins*, Studies in the Dead Sea Scrolls and Related Literature (Grand Rapids, MI; Cambridge, UK: William B. Eerdmans Publishing Company, 2000), 78, n.14.

And He shall judge the poor with righteousness and he shall decide the equity for *the poor of the land*, and he shall strike *the land* with the rod of his mouth and with the breath of his lips he shall kill the wicked.

The issue is the addition of articles on the word ארץ in the Scroll i.e., לעגוי הארץ (for the poor of the land) and הכהו ארעה (and he shall strike the land). Pulikottil argues that this addition of the article may be due to conceptual inclination of the scribe regarding "the land."[39] Moreover, this could be exegetical addition to the body of the text.[40] For example, in 11:1-9, there are three occurrences of the word ארץ out of which in v. 4 there are two occurrences without definite article. The third one occurs at v. 9 with definite article which is the climax of this pericope. Moreover, verse 9 talks about *the land* being filled with the knowledge of the LORD. So, it is clear that the addition of definite article in v. 4 is a case of conceptual harmonization in the light of v. 9. However, the concept of land is not the only idea behind the scribe's modification here. In the light of v.1 which talks about "shoot of Jesse" צמח/חטר is a messianic figure who would judge and smite the earth and kill the wicked (v.4). Swarup notes that this idea of triumphant messiah, son of David is shared idea in Jewish and Qumran expectation.[41] Therefore, the Scroll explicitly emphasizes the role of "shoot of Jesse" who is the expected Messiah and his influence on the land whereas MT

---

[39] Pulikottil, *Transmission of Biblical Texts*, 74.

[40] Tov, *Textual Criticism of the Hebrew Bible*, 260.

[41] Swarup, *The Self-Understanding of the Dead Sea Scrolls Community*, 131.

implicitly envisions the same. So, the distinct messianic idea of the Scroll here has to do with צמח/חטר and the land.

Isaiah 11:9

MT

לֹא־יָרֵעוּ וְלֹא־יַשְׁחִיתוּ בְּכָל־הַר קָדְשִׁי כִּי־מָלְאָה

הָאָרֶץ דֵּעָה אֶת־יְהוָה כַּמַּיִם לַיָּם מְכַסִּים: פ

They will not hurt and destroy all my holy mountain, for the earth shall be full of knowledge of the LORD, as the waters cover the sea.

Scroll

לוא ירעו ולוא ישחיתו בכל הר קדשי כי תמלאה

הארץ דעה את יהוה כמים לײם מכססים

They will not hurt and destroy all my holy mountain, *for the earth shall be full of knowledge of the LORD*, as the waters cover the sea.

The issue is change of tense from perfect to imperfect in the Scroll. The Scribe of the Scroll reads this verse in futuristic sense. Watts translates this as "shall have become full."[42] Similarly, Wildberger reads this in imperfect sense and translates the same as "will have become full."[43] Pulikottil considers this as historical exegesis where the scribe is concerned with the historical correctness.[44] Rubinstein notes

---

[42] Watts, *Isaiah 1-33*, 168–69.

[43] Wildberger, *Isaiah 1-12*, 462.

[44] Pulikottil, *Transmission of Biblical Texts*, 133–34.

that the tendency to use imperfect for the MT perfect reflects an early tradition to read the verbs in futuristic sense.[45] In the light of the previous unique readings (v.1 and v. 4) the Scroll's interprets the eschatological messianic age has not yet arrived by changing the tense of the verb from perfect to imperfect.[46] The distinct messianic idea of the Scroll here has to do with "age to come" i.e., messianic age—an aspect well attested in the Qumran literature which will be dealt in the following chapter.

Isaiah 26

Isaiah 26:8

MT

אַף אֹרַח מִשְׁפָּטֶיךָ יְהוָה קִוִּינוּךָ לְשִׁמְךָ וּלְזִכְרְךָ תַּאֲוַת־נָפֶשׁ׃

Indeed, in the path of your judgment, O LORD! We wait for you, your name and your memory is the desire of the soul.

Scroll

אף ארח משפטיך   יהוה קוינו לשמך ולתורתך תאות נפש

Indeed, in the path of your judgments, O LORD! *We wait.* Your name and *your Law* are the desire of the soul

---

[45] Arie Rubinstein, "Notes on the Use of the Tenses in the Variant Readings of the Isaiah Scroll," *VT* 3.1 (1953): 93.

[46] In MT the tense of the verb can be taken as prophetic perfect. However, the Scroll must be using earlier traditions as Rubinstein suggested in his article.

There are three issues here. First, there is a long space after משפטיך which may be due to versification by the scribe. Second one, the Scroll reads קוינו (we wait) for MT's קִוִּינוּךָ (we wait for you). Thirdly, the Scroll replaces the word וּלְזִכְרְךָ (and your reading memory) with ולתורתך (and your reading law). Pulikottil offers two possible explanations for this scribal modification. First, the change on the verb קוה may be to avoid the interpretation that people waiting for YHWH.[47] The intention behind this change could be to protect the honor of God. Secondly, in order to protect the honor of God, the Scribe made indirect reference to שם (name) and then paralleled with תורה (Law).[48] Pulikottil points to the significance of Torah in the scribal change here. Earlier in 2:3, it is already noted the Torah has messianic significance where 'they' are responsible to teach the Law. This teaching of the Law is one of the messianic responsibilities. Keeping this in mind, it is possible that this unique reading not only reflects significance of *Torah* but also significance of Messiah in relation to *Torah*.

Isaiah 40

Isaiah 40:5

The issue here is regarding the word יחד. The Scroll reads as יחדיו for יַחְדָּו in MT.[49] The Scroll reads it as plural suffix

---

[47] Pulikottil, *Transmission of Biblical Texts*, 145.

[48] Cf. Deut 28:58, and 62:2 where parallelism between תורה and שם occurs.

[49] Cf. Isa 41:1, 20, 23; 43:9, 17; 45:16, 21; 46:2; 48:13; 52:8, 9; 60:13; and 66:17

which is a plene form. According to Pulikottil, the scribe of the Scroll changed this word whenever there is a possibility of reading it as a noun, or object or possible subject of condemnatory action.[50] So, the scribe, in such cases changed to adverb form to avoid any misinterpretation of the word. This word is well attested in the Yaḥad documents such as CD, 1QS, 1QSᵃ, ᵇ, 1QM and *Pesharim*.[51] Talmon notes that such documents preserve "diverse factions of Jewry in the outgoing Second Temple Period."[52] Moreover, the Yaḥad saw themselves as messianic community in waiting for the age to come in this verse.[53] In that the glory of the LORD will be revealed and the Yaḥad would be receptors of such revelation in the age to come. This is a futuristic reading which indicates an eschatological age. This can be considered as messianic age (cf. Isa 11:9 and 2:3). Therefore, the unique reading at Isa 40:5 reflects the messianic sensibilities of the Yaḥad community. The distinct messianic idea of the Scroll here is the self-understanding of community as messianic community which also is attested in the Qumran scrolls.

Isaiah 42

In Isa 42:1 is a unique reading that reflects a distinct messianic ideology regarding הוהי דבע (Servant of the LORD).

---

[50] Pulikottil, *Transmission of Biblical Texts*, 172.

[51] Pulikottil, *Transmission of Biblical Texts,* 166.

[52] Shemaryahu Talmon, "The Concept of Māšîah and Messianism in Early Judaism," in *The Messiah: Developments in Earliest Judaism and Christianity* (Minneapolis: Fortress Pr, 1992), 101.

[53] Talmon, "The Concept of Māšîah and Messianism in Early Judaism." 104.

Isaiah 42:1

MT

הֵן עַבְדִּי אֶתְמָד־בּוֹ בְּחִירִי רָצְתָה נַפְשִׁי
נָתַתִּי רוּחִי עָלָיו מִשְׁפָּט לַגּוֹיִם יוֹצִיא:

Behold! My servant whom I uphold; my chosen in whom I delight; I will put my spirit on him, and he will bring justice to the nations.

Scroll

הנה עבדי אתמוכה בו בחירי רצתה נפשי
נתתי רוחי עליו משפטו לגואים יוציא

Behold! My servant whom I uphold; my chosen in whom I delight; I will put my spirit on him, and he will bring *his* justice to the nations.

The issue is regarding pronominal suffix on the noun משפט. The Scroll renders third masculine singular pronominal suffix which reads as "and his justice." The same phenomenon has been observed in 9:5. This type change may be regarded as exegetical interpolation as it brings a new meaning to the text. The interpretative difference between the Scroll and MT is that the former understands the responsibility of עבד (Servant) to judge the nations depends on his own discretion. However, in the later, the responsibility depends on both YHWH and his servant. For Chamberlain the Scroll's reading expresses heightened authority of the servant and indicates that it reflects a legal and judicial role of Messiah.[54] Moreover, Collins points out that this verse is interpreted messianically in the Targum.[55] On the other hand, Pulikottil notes that the Scroll's reading reflect a "distinct messianic ideology."[56] Therefore, this unique reading has messianic significance which is different from MT. The distinct messianic idea of the Scroll here is the legal and judicial role of servant messiah. This aspect will be explored in the next chapter where there is a distinct messianic ideology regarding the Servant Songs.

Isaiah 49

There are two unique readings that reflect messianic sensibilities of the Scroll

Isaiah 49:2

MT

וַיָּשֶׂם פִּי כְּחֶרֶב חַדָּה בְּצֵל יָדוֹ הֶחְבִּיאָנִי

וַיְשִׂימֵנִי לְחֵץ בָּרוּר בְּאַשְׁפָּתוֹ הִסְתִּירָנִי:

He made my mouth like a sharp sword, in the shadow of his hand he hid me, he made me a polish arrow, in his quiver he hid me away

The issue here is that the Scroll renders as חרב׳ for כחרב. The issue here is that כ has been added supralinearly.

---

⁵⁴ Chamberlain, "Functions of God as Messianic Titles in the Complete Qumran Isaiah Scroll," 369.

⁵⁵ Collins, *The Scepter and the Star*, 143.

⁵⁶ Pulikottil, *Transmission of Biblical Texts*, 149.

Pulikottil points out to the possibility of more than one scribe working on the Scroll.[57] He further notes that the dropping of the preposition "כְּ" forms a unique expression.[58] According to Goldingay and Payne the preposition here in the Scroll is not used as comparison but to indicate identity.[59] It seems originally the Scroll understood "the mouth" to be sharp sword but later on the preposition was added to bring a comparison. Whatever the case may be, the Scroll definitely deviates from MT in its interpretation. In that originally the Scroll seems to understand "mouth" prophet's tool of acting (cf. Ps 57:5- ולשונם חרחב הדבר - and their tongues sharp swords). Conversely, 'prophet' is considered as messiah in Qumran literature. Moreover, this unique reading points to the prophetic role of the Servant which may involve teaching function. Therefore, this unique reading does reflect messianic understanding of the Scroll. The distinct messianic idea of the Scroll projected here is the role of the servant as a prophet and teacher.

Isaiah 49:6

MT

וַיֹּאמֶר נָקֵל מִהְיוֹתְךָ לִי עֶבֶד לְהָקִים אֶת־שִׁבְטֵי יַעֲקֹב [כ= וּנְצִירֵי] [ק= וּנְצוּרֵי] יִשְׂרָאֵל לְהָשִׁיב וּנְתַתִּיךָ לְאוֹר גּוֹיִם לִהְיוֹת יְשׁוּעָתִי עַד־קְצֵה הָאָרֶץ: ס

---

[57] Pulikottil, *Transmission of Biblical Texts*, 67.

[58] Pulikottil, *Transmission of Biblical Texts.* 67.

[59] Goldingay and Payne, *Isaiah 40-55*, 157.

He says, 'it is too light a thing that you should be my servant to raise up the tribes of Jacob and to restore the survivors of Israel; I will give you as a light to the nations, that my salvation may reach to the end of the earth.'

Scroll

ויואמר נקל מהיותך לי עבד להקים את שבטי ישראל ונצירי

יעקוב להשיב ונתתיך לאור גוים להיות ישועתי עד קצה הארץ

He says, 'it is too light a thing that you should be my servant to raise the *shoots of Israel and the survivors of Jacob,* I will give you as a light to the nations, that my salvation may reach to the end of the earth.'

The issue is regarding the inversion of יעקוב and ישראל in the Scroll. Pulikottil notes that the expression שבטי יעקוב is a unique expression here in MT.[60] Goldingay and Payne notes that such a reverse order may be due to scribe's concern for the familiar expressions שבטי ישראל (clans of Israel) which occurs in Gen 49:16 and 28.[61] Moreover the expression "shoots/clans of Israel" occurs here and in 63:17. The expression "clans of Jacob" on the other hand does not occur anywhere in OT. Gerhard von Rad argues that this could be an anti-thesis between old clan alliance and national identity of Israel.[62] However, the expression שבטי ישראל has to be understood

---

[60] Pulikottil, *Transmission of Biblical Texts*, 68.

[61] John Goldingay and David Payne, *Isaiah 40-55* (ICC 2; NY: T. & T. Clark International, 2006), 165.

[62] Gerhard von Rad, *Old Testament Theology* (trans. D. M. G. Stalker; vol. 2; New York: Harper and Row, 1966), 253.

in connection with נצירי יעקוב (remnant of Jacob). If we closely examine the verse, *Kethib* has וּנְצִירֵי which is an adjective masculine plural construct whereas *Qere* has וּנְצִירֵי which is Qal Passive Participle masculine plural construct. Goldingay and Payne suggest that it is plausible that *Kethib's hapax legomenon* indicates the meaning of "branch/shoot" rather than preserve.[63] If this argument is accepted then the word נצר in this verse does give some messianic sense (cf. 11:1). Moreover, the word נצר for Swarup carries a collective identity of the DSS community.[64] The words שבט and נצר has messianic significance in the Qumran literature. Therefore, the unique reading here has messianic significance. The interpretative difference is that the Scroll explicitly expresses that promise of restoration is transferred to "shoots of Israel" (שבט) to the entire Jewish people (נצר).[65] This is the distinct messianic idea of the Scroll here.

Isaiah 50

There are two unique readings that reflect messianic ideology.

Isaiah 50:4

MT

אֲדֹנָי יְהֹוִה נָתַן לִי לְשׁוֹן לִמּוּדִים לָדַעַת לָעוּת

אֶת־יָעֵף דָּבָר יָעִיר בַּבֹּקֶר בַּבֹּקֶר יָעִיר לִי אֹזֶן לִשְׁמֹעַ כַּלִּמּוּדִים:

---

[63] Michaelis as cited by Goldingay and Payne, *Isaiah 40-55*, vol. II, 165.

[64] Swarup, *The Self-Understanding of the Dead Sea Scrolls Community*, 44.

[65] Collins, *The Scepter and the Star*, 32.

The LORD God has given to me the tongue of a teacher to know to help the weary *with* a word. He awakens in the morning by morning; he awakens my ear to heed as students.

Scroll

אדוני יהוה נתן לי לשון למודים לדעת לעות את יעף דב[ר] ויעיר

בבוקר בבוקר ויעיר לי אתן לשמוע כלמודים

The LORD God has given me the tongue of a teacher to know to help the weary *with word and* he awakens in the morning by morning *and* he awakens my ear to heed as students.

The issue here is the addition of *waw*-conjunction at יעיר which occurs two times in the text in the Scroll. BHS proposes to delete one occurrence. Pulikottil notes that the first *waw* that has been added by the scribe is for the purpose of punctuation.[66] In that it clarifies the relationship of דבר to the rest of the sentence. The second *waw* is an epexegetical *waw*.[67] The purpose of epexegetical *waw* is to restate or paraphrase the previous line. D. W. Baker suggests that the occurrence of *waw-explicativum* is very common in Biblical Hebrew and warns against haste in emending the text wherever *waw-explicativum* occurs thinking that is a gloss.[68] On the other hand, Watts translates דבר adverbially

---

[66] Pulikottil, *Transmission of Biblical Texts*, 95.

[67] An epexegetical waw is used to introduce a clause by paraphrasing the previous clause, see, Bruce K. Waltke and M. O'Connor, *An Introduction to Biblical Hebrew Syntax* (Winona Lake, Indiana: 1990), 653.

[68] David W Baker, "Further Examples of the Wāw Explicativum," *VT* 30.2 (1980): 134.

as "with or by word."[69] It seems that MT is linking the word דבר with what precedes which the Scroll makes it explicit by adding *waw*.[70] It is quite possible for this verse to have messianic significance because the addition of the second *waw* does effect the interpretation of the text. Moreover, Michael O. Wise presents a "maximalist view" of allusions to the Servant Songs and in that like Servant, the Teacher in the Qumran literature claims to be empowered by the Spirit and has "teacher's tongue."[71] Since this epexegetical *waw* defines the various elements in the text, it follows that the Scribe of the Scroll made this changes keeping in mind the entrusted mission of the servant. In that the Scroll intensifies the fact that it was God who would grant his עבד a tongue of a teacher. Furthermore, the Servant is seen as a student who is taught by God to encourage the weary. On the other hand, in MT the role of God in Servant's mission is implicitly assumed. Therefore, the Scroll here projects a distinct messianic idea of God endowing and teaching the Servant would in turn carry out the function of a Teacher and herald of peace.

Isaiah 50:8

The Scroll reads יחדיו with a plural suffix for MT's יַחַד. This change is similar to 40:5 which has already been dealt. The Scroll here, like in 40:5, saw the possibility of understanding this word as the object of עמד (to stand) which is a verb. So,

---

[69] Watts, *Isaiah 34-66*, 196.

[70] Goldingay and Payne, *Isaiah 40-55*, vol. II, 208.

[71] Michael O Wise, *The First Messiah* (San Francisco: HarperSan Francisco, 1999), 290.

he changes it to mean adverbially as "together." As already noted earlier the Scroll understands this word in a special way and is parallel to other Qumran texts in which this word is associated with the community. Moreover, this word represents collective concept of Israel as עבד־יהוה (Servant of the LORD). This notion, according to Swarup not only applied to the Messiah but also to the entire community.[72] Therefore, this unique reading too carries a distinct messianic idea of the self-understanding of yaḥad as a messianic community which is attested in the Qumran literature.

Isaiah 52:13- 53

Isaiah 52:14

MT

כַּאֲשֶׁר שָׁמְמוּ עָלֶיךָ רַבִּים כֵּן־מִשְׁחַת מֵאִישׁ מַרְאֵהוּ וְתֹאֲרוֹ מִבְּנֵי אָדָם:

Just as they were many who were appalled at you, his appearance was disfigured beyond that of men and his form beyond the sons of man.

Scroll

כאשר שממו רבים כן משחתי מאישמראהו ותוארו מבני האדם

Just as they were many who were appalled at you, I *anointed* his appearance beyond that of men and his form beyond the sons of man.

The Scroll reads משחתי —a perfect verb form for MT's משחת. This is a case of root substitution. MT uses √שחת

---

[72] Swarup, *The Self-Understanding of the Dead Sea Scrolls Community*, 49.

(marred) whereas the Scroll substitutes with √משח (to anoint).[73] On the other hand LXX reads ἀδοξήσει which may be translated as "he will be without glory." Targum uses the word חשור which may be translated as "was wretched" from the √שוח which means "sink down or be depressed." On the other hand, J. Reider suggests that the extra *yod* added is similar to Hos 10:11 (אהבתי).[74] However this is a very remote to the present text as the Scribe might have been influenced by the concept of עבד יהוה (Servant of the LORD).[75] Brownlee while assuming the correctness of vocalization of MT מִשְׁחַת, points out to the syntactical difficulty in its relation with מן.[76] The Scroll attempted to clarify this ambiguity. Furthermore, Brownlee points to the verbal harmonization between Dan 8:24-25 with Isa 52:14.[77] Here in these texts the same √שחת is used. This shows that MT is indicative of suffering aspect of the Servant whereas the Scroll emphasizes anointing aspect of the Servant. The anointing aspect of the Servant is resonating with Qumran understanding which will be dealt in the following chapter. The distinct idea of the Scroll is anointing of the Messiah.

---

[73] Pulikottil, *Transmission of Biblical Texts*, 152.

[74] J. Reider, "On MSHTY Int He Qumran Scrolls," *BASOR* 134 (1954): 27–28.

[75] Pulikottil, *Transmission of Biblical Texts*, 153.

[76] W. H. Brownlee, "The Servant of the LORD in the Qumran Scrolls I," *BASOR* 132 (1953): 11.

[77] Brownlee, "The Servant of the LORD in the Qumran Scrolls I." 13.

Isaiah 61

Isaiah 61:1

MT

רוּחַ אֲדֹנָי יְהוִה עָלָי יַעַן מָשַׁח יְהוָה אֹתִי לְבַשֵּׂר עֲנָוִים שְׁלָחַנִי
לַחֲבֹשׁ לְנִשְׁבְּרֵי־לֵב לִקְרֹא לִשְׁבוּיִם דְּרוֹר וְלַאֲסוּרִים פְּקַח־קוֹחַ:

The Spirit of the LORD God is up on me, because the LORD
has anointed me to bring glad tidings to the oppressed, He
sent me, to bind the broken-hearted, to proclaim liberty to
the captives, and to release to the prisoners.

Scroll

רוח יהוה עלי יען משח יהוה אותי לבשר ענוים ולחבוש
לנשביר לב לקרוא לשבויים דרור ולאסורים פקחקוח

The Spirit of the LORD is upon me, because the LORD has
anointed me to bring glad tidings to the oppressed he sent
me, *and* to bind up the broken-hearted, to proclaim liberty
to the captives and release to the prisoners.

There are two significant issues here.[78] Scroll adds *waw*
at לחבוש (to bind or heal) and original omission of the verb
שלחתי (to send).[79] The addition of *waw* has explicative effect

---

[78] The word אדני is omitted in the Scroll because the Scribe's familiarity
with the common biblical phrases רוח יהוה.

[79] שלחתי supralineally added above לחבוש, see, Donald W. Parry and
Elisha Qimron, eds., *The Great Isaiah Scroll (1QIsaa)* (STDJ XXXII; Leiden:
Brill, 1999), 100.

and the original omission is very significant syntactically. The addition of the *waw* properly punctuates the sentence in a way that the infinitives are dependent on the verb משח (to anoint). On the other hand, the original omission of the verb שלחתי further clarifies this aspect. This means that in MT the infinitive of חבוש is dependent on the verb.[80] In the Scroll the addition of *waw* and the omission of שלחתי make the infinitives לחבוש (to bring glad tidings), לנשביר (to bind up), לקרוא (to proclaim), and לשבויים (to release) dependent with the verb משח (to anoint). It is clear that the scribal changes here have to do with the concept of "anointing and the anointed one" and the tasks of the anointed. Therefore, this is the distinct messianic idea of the Scroll and the unique reading here reflects messianic significance.

Isaiah 61:3

MT

לָשׂוּם לַאֲבֵלֵי צִיּוֹן לָתֵת לָהֶם פְּאֵר תַּחַת אֵפֶר שֶׁמֶן שָׂשׂוֹן תַּחַת אֵבֶל

מַעֲטֵה תְהִלָּה תַּחַת רוּחַ כֵּהָה וְקֹרָא לָהֶם אֵילֵי הַצֶּדֶק מַטַּע יְהוָה לְהִתְפָּאֵר:

To provide the mourners of Zion, to give to them garland instead of ash, the oil of gladness instead of mourning, garment of praise instead of a spirit of despair. And it will be called the oaks of righteousness, planting of the LORD, in order to display splendour.

---

[80] Pulikottil, *Transmission of Biblical Texts*, 85.

Scroll

לשום לאבילי ציון לתת להמה אפד שמן ששמן ששון תחת אבל

מעטה תהלה תחת רוח כהה וקראו להמה אילי הצדק מטע יהוה להתפאר

To provide the mourners of Zion, to give to them a garland instead of ash, the oil of gladness instead of mourning, garment of praise instead of a spirit of despair, And *they will be called* as oaks of righteousness, planting of the LORD, in order to display splendor.

The issue is regarding the verb קרא. In MT it is vocalized as וְקֹרָא which Pual w/c Perfect third masculine singular ק רא√ which means "to call or to be called." However, the Scroll reads וקראו which could be Pual w/c 3mpl "they will be called." Pulikottil considers this as a grammatical harmonization by the scribe as the antecedent of this verb is לאבילי ציון (mourners of Zion).[81] This change by the Scribe has explicative significance. In the light of this change, and in relation to the phrase מטע יהוה (planting of the LORD), the mourners of Zion are the planting of the LORD—the remnant. In the DSS community, "planting of the LORD" reflect their self-understanding as "eternal plant-righteous remnant."[82] This idea of remnant carries messianic significance as the community considers themselves as a messianic community in whom God will be glorified.[83] The corporate idea of community as messianic is a distinct messianic idea

---

[81] Pulikottil, *Transmission of Biblical Texts,* 129.

[82] Swarup, *The Self-Understanding of the Dead Sea Scrolls Community,* 21.

[83] Swarup, *The Self-Understanding of the Dead Sea Scrolls Community,* 21.

in the Scroll which is well attested in the Qumran literature. Therefore, the unique reading here reflects messianic significance.

Isaiah 62

Isaiah 62:11

MT

הִנֵּה יְהוָה הִשְׁמִיעַ אֶל־קְצֵה הָאָרֶץ אִמְרוּ לְבַת־צִיּוֹן
הִנֵּה יִשְׁעֵךְ בָּא הִנֵּה שְׂכָרוֹ אִתּוֹ וּפְעֻלָּתוֹ לְפָנָיו:

Behold! The LORD has proclaimed to the end of the earth, say to the daughter of Zion, 'Behold your salvation comes; his reward is with him! His recompense is before him.'

Scroll

הנה יהוה השמיעו אל קצוי הארץ אמורו לבת ציון הנה
ישעך בא הנה שכרו אתו ופעלתיו לפניו

Behold! The LORD has *summoned him* to the ends of the earth, say to the daughter of Zion, Behold! Your salvation comes, behold his reward is with him, and his recompense is before him.'

The issue is with the word הִשְׁמִיעַ.[84] The Scroll reads as השמיעו (he summoned him) which may be vocalized as an imperative to mean "summoned him." Pulikottil points to Brownlee's suggestion that the 'him' of "summoned him' is the messianic servant of the LORD who has been addressed to

---

[84] Hiph Pft third masculine singular √שמע "to hear."

the mount Zion and the same is mentioned as "Salvation."[85] This same phenomenon is identified by Chamberlain in Isa. 51:5 where ישעי (my deliverance), תורה (Law), משפטי (my judgment), צדקי (my righteousness), and ישועתי (my salvation) are personified as the agent of God and used as messianic titles.[86] Keeping this in mind, while MT does not read this verse messianically, the Scroll does. The messianic titles are well attested in the Qumran literature which will be dealt in the next chapter. Therefore, this unique reading has messianic significance. The distinct messianic idea of the Scroll points to salvafic task of the Servant of the LORD.

Conclusion

The above analysis affirmed that there are unique readings in the Scroll that reflect distinct messianic idea of the Scroll. From the above analysis the following are the distinct messianic ideas of the Scroll: 1) Warrior Messiah (Isa 1:24; 10:24); 2) Messianic Teacher at the end of days (Isa 2:23; 26:8); 3) Self-understanding of community as messianic (Isa 4:2; 11:4, 61:3); 4) Messiah as Son of God (Isa 7:14; 9:5-6); 5) Messianic age (Isa 11:9); 6) יחד as Messianic community (Isa 40:5; 50:8); 7) Messianic Servant (Isa 42:1; 49:2, 6; 50:4, 52:14; 61:1; 62:11). Based on these messianic ideas, the messianic milieu of the Scroll will be identified in the following chapter.

---

[85] Brownlee, *The Meaning of the Qumran Scrolls for the Bible: With Special Attention to the Book of Isaiah,* 201; Pulikottil, *Transmission of Biblical Texts,* 153.

[86] Chamberlain, "Functions of God as Messianic Titles in the Complete Qumran Isaiah Scroll," 366.

Chapter 3

Messianic Milieu of the Scroll

The messianic significance of the unique readings of the Scroll resonates with the יחד documents and in particular more inclined to 1QS messianic sensibilities. With this hypothesis in mind, this chapter attempts to locate messianic milieu of the Scroll. In order to do that first, harmonization method which is part of textual method will be employed by which ideological affinities between the Scroll and other biblical and Qumran literature will be identified. Secondly, the varied messianic ideologies as reflected by some of the unique readings will be analyzed to find out whether these ideologies correspond to Yaḥad community and in particular to 1QS.

Harmonization Method

The messianic significance of the unique readings can be identified by harmonization method. This research understands that all scribal modification may not be due to scribal errors. The modifications may have been motivated by textual, contextual, and theological framework of the scribe of the scroll. Keeping this in mind, unique readings will be analyzed using harmonization method in order to find if there are any distinct messianic ideas that resonate with Qumran literature. It is to be noted that an analysis of unique readings for distinct messianic ideas of the other ancient texts may not always be textual harmony but also it could be conceptual affinity. Ronald S. Hendel notes that unique divergences which may be errors or innovations points to only one text and does not point to any textual relationships.[1] However, unique divergences may not necessarily indicate textual relationship but may be indicative of conceptual affinity with other texts. Furthermore, this method helps to locate ideological milieu of the Scroll. In this case, the messianic milieu of the Scroll may be identified.

Emanuel Tov defines harmonization as "secondary approximation of details."[2] In other words harmonizations are adaptations of different textual elements in a verse, sentence, chapter, in the same book or different books. These harmonizations can be distinguished as within the same context, same book or different books.[3] Pulikottil distinguishes the same as contextual, textual, and intertextual harmonizations. Most of the harmonizations are intentional though there may be unintentional as well.[4]

---

[1] Ronald S. Hendel, "Assessing the Text-Critical Theories of the Hebrew Bible after Qumran," in *The Oxford Handbook of the Dead Sea Scrolls* (ed. John J. Collins and Timothy H. Lim; Oxford: Oxford Univ Pr, 2010), 283.

[2] Tov, "The Nature and Backgrounds of Harmonizations in Biblical Manuscripts," 3.

[3] Tov, "The Nature and Backgrounds of Harmonizations in Biblical Manuscripts." 5.

[4] Tov, *Textual Criticism of the Hebrew Bible*, 258.

There are three types of harmonizations as indicated before. For example, first, contextual harmonizations are influenced by the immediate context of the reading. They can be identified by looking at addition of the words, prepositional changes, and root substitutions, substitutions in case of *hapax legomenon,* accusative marker additions, and modification involving divine names.[5] Secondly, textual harmonizations are influenced by other passages from the same book. They can be identified by looking at grammatical and conceptual concerns, avoidance of contradictions, and concern of biblical phraseology.[6] Thirdly intertextual harmonizations are influenced by other books of the bible or any other books outside the book (as in the case of the Scroll). They can be identified by looking at verbal harmonizations, conceptual adaptations based on popular biblical idioms, concepts, and phraseology, thematic harmonizations, and modernizations.[7]

Another method of harmonization is rabbinic exegetical technique called הוש הריזג. G. J. Brooke points out that this is a rabbinic method in which "biblical verses can be juxtaposed in commentary or interpretation simply because they share a common word or two."[8]

---

[5] Pulikottil, *Transmission of Biblical Texts,* 50–54.

[6] Pulikottil, *Transmission of Biblical Texts,* 55-68.

[7] Pulikottil, *Transmission of Biblical Texts,* 64-71.

[8] George J Brooke, *Exegesis at Qumran: 4QFlorilegium in Its Jewish Context,* JSOTSup 29 (Sheffield: JSOT Pr, 1985), 23.

E.g.: 1 Samuel 1:22

MT

וַיָשַׁב שָׁם עַד־עוֹלָם ⁹

And he must stay there forever[10]

4QSamᵃ

+ עד עולם ונת] תיהו נזיר עד עולם כול ימי [חייו

+ ...forever and I shall dedicate him as a nazir forever all the days of [his life...

Tov considers this as a midrashic-like addition in which this addition was motivated by the word נזיר which actually occurs only in Ben Sira 46:13, Num 6, Judg 13:5, 7.[11] This word does not occur in *MT* and *LXX*. So, the scribe of the 4QSamᵃ under the theological influence of concept נזיר harmonizes the text of Samuel which resonates with Ben Sria and other Bible passages as noted above.

The above method will be employed to find out ideological affinities as resonated by the unique readings with other Qumran and biblical documents. In doing so, the messianic milieu may be identified.

---

⁹ Agrees with LXX.

¹⁰ Translation is by the researcher unless it is indicated otherwise.

¹¹ Tov, *Textual Criticism of the Hebrew Bible*, 261.

Messianic Milieu of the Scroll

Ideological Affinities with other Biblical and Qumran Literature

Warrior Messiah

The messianic idea of the Scroll at 1:24 resonates with the "warrior Messiah" of the Rule of War (1QM). Chamberlain understand the antecedent of third masculine singular pronominal suffix as "Righteousness" and suggests that this has corporate understanding of the Sect per se.[12] Moreover the usage of third masculine singular pronominal suffix with the word משיח is well attested in CD 2:12 and 5:21-6:1.[13] This refers to the closeness of God with "His Messiah" who would act on his behalf to crush his enemies. In addition to this, Chamberlain, further notes that the Scroll understood v. 24 as the promise of God who fight the enemies of Messiah within Zion.[14]

The connection between Messiah and his enemies is well attested in the War rule (1QM). However, there are scholars who argue that there is no messianic significance of 1QM. For example, William Sanford Lasor argues that 1QM has no messianic significance.[15] However, the mention of the

---

[12] Chamberlain, "Functions of God as Messianic Titles in the Complete Qumran Isaiah Scroll," 371.

[13] J. R. Samuel Raj, *The "Anointed Ones" in the Qumran Literature* (Delhi: ISPCK, 2005), 27.

[14] Chamberlain, "Functions of God as Messianic Titles in the Complete Qumran Isaiah Scroll," 371.

[15] William Sanford La Sor, "'Messiahs of Aaron and Israel,'" *VT* 6.4 (1956): 210.

word מָשִׁיחַ with a plural suffix (the anointed ones) occurs at 1QM 11: 7. Karl Georg Kuhn understands the "anointed ones" as the prophets of OT (cf. Isa 49:2).[16] Furthermore, he correlates 1QM 11:7 with Ps. 105:15 as pointing out to OT scheme of redemption through David, King, and the anointed ones.[17] On the other hand, R. E. Brown argues that the Scroll does project messianic significance and that it endorses the Aaronids superiority though the whole community is involved in the battle.[18] In fact, he points that there is a possibility of "Messiah of Israel" as some of the columns of the Scroll are incomplete. This "Messiah of Israel" is none other than "נשיא" (the leader or the Prince of the Congregation).[19] This argument is plausible as the priest do not defile themselves with the bloodshed in the battle. Furthermore, the Prince is implicitly mentioned in 1QM 11:6-7 as "שבט מישראל" (Scepter of Israel). The same figure also occurs in CD 7:18-21 as "Prince of Congregation" with the military function. Therefore, "Prince" in 1QM 5:1-2 is Messiah of Israel. Moreover, 1QM 12:9b-15 has a very close conceptual harmony with the Scroll. In that the figure "גבור" (Warrior) is seen with the military function who would crush and smite his enemies and nations. This military function has messianic connotation.[20]

---

[16] Karl G Kuhn, "The Two Messiahs of Aaron and Israel," in *The Scrolls and the New Testament* (New York: Crossroad, 1992), 59–60.

[17] Kuhn, "The Two Messiahs of Aaron and Israel." 60.

[18] Raymond Edward Brown, "Messianism of QumrâN," *CBQ* 19.1 (1957): 58.

[19] Brown, "Messianism of QumrâN." 58.

[20] F. F. Bruce, *Biblical Exegesis in the Qumran Texts* (London: The Tyndale Press, 1960), 52.

1QM 12:9b-11:

קומה גבור שבה שביכה איש כבוד ושול שללכה עושי חיל. תן

ידכה בעורף אויביכה ורגלכה על במותי חלל. מחץ גוים צריכה וחרבכה...

Rise up Hero! Lead off thy captives O Glorious One! Gather up thy spoils, O Author of mighty deeds! Lay thy hands on the neck of thine *enemies*, and thy feet on the pile of the slain! Smite the nations, thy *adversaries*...[21]

The above verse has some textual harmony with Isa 1:24. In that the nouns "צר" (adversary) and "איב" (enemy) occurs here in 1QM 12:9b-11. Samuel Raj on the other hand, notes that this "גבור" (warrior) is synonymous to Prince and Messiah of Israel in 1QM.[22] So, the scribal modification at Isa 1:24 the distinct messianic idea of "warrior Messiah" is well attested in 1QM. The conceptual harmony between the 1:24 and 1QM pointed to the understanding of an eschatological war in which "Messiah of Israel" would have a military role to crush enemies.[23] Therefore, the messianic significance of the unique reading at Isa 1:24 resonate with the messianic expectation of the 1QM.

---

[21] Geza Vermes, *The Complete Dead Sea Scrolls in English* (rev.; England: Penguin books, 2004), 178.

[22] Samuel Raj, *The "Anointed Ones" in the Qumran Literature*, 87.

[23] Collins argues that the same phenomenon is echoed in fragmentary document 4Q285 War Rule in which the reference to צמח דויד (branch of David) harmonized with Isaiah 11. This "branch" is associated with the Prince in 4Q285 who would strike the earth with the rod of his mouth and kill the wicked. He further notes that such a correlation of various epithets and titles may be applied in the interpretation of the scrolls, see, Collins, *The Scepter and the Star*, 64–67.

The unique reading at 10:24 also reflects the understanding of "Warrior Messiah." This verse specifically talks about exhortation of the people of Zion, encouraging them not to worry about the rod of Assyria. The idea here reflects CD 7:20:

מישראל השבט הוא נשיא כל העדה ובעמדו וקרקר

The Scepter is the Prince of all congregation, and when he comes he shall smite all the children of Seth.[24]

This above text has some allusions with Num 24:17:

וְקָם שֵׁבֶט מִיִּשְׂרָאֵל וּמָחַץ פַּאֲתֵי מוֹאָב וְקַרְקַר כָּל־בְּנֵי־שֵׁת:

And a Scepter will rise out of Israel, and it shall crush the borderlines of Moab, and all the sons of Seth.

There is the reference to שבט in the above texts. In 10:24 this word is contrasted with YHWH מטה (rod) in Isa 10:26.[25] In that the Lord's staff (הטמ) will overcome the waters and the people of Israel need not to be afraid of Assyria's rod (שבט). Samuel Raj points that this word שבט (Scepter) occurs in 1QM 11:6-7 which is a citation from Num 24:17.[26] It also occurs in CD 7:18-21 where there is a clear reference to the Prince as שבט (Scepter) who would crush the children of Seth.[27] In other words, this messianic figure can be considered as "a warrior messiah" for his militant function.

---

[24] Maurya P Horgan, *Pesharim: Qumran Interpretations of Biblical Books* (CBQMS 8; Washington DC.: Catholic Biblical Assoc, 1979), 79; Vermes, *The Complete Dead Sea Scrolls in English*, 135.

[25] מַטֶּה is synonym to שֵׁבֶט, see, David J. A. Clines, ed., *DCH* V: 237.

[26] Samuel Raj, *The "Anointed Ones" in the Qumran Literature*, 85–86.

[27] Collins, *The Scepter and the Star*, 72–73.

Messianic Teacher at the end of days

The unique readings of the Scroll at Isa 2:3 and 26:8 reflects the concept of Messianic Teacher at the end of days in the Damascus Document (CD). The reference to 'they' in the Scroll may refer to either "Interpreter of the Law" of the past or Teacher of Righteousness who comes at the end of days. The unique reading at Isa 2:3 has some allusions to CD 6:7-11.

CD 6:7-11:

והמחוקק הוא דורש התורה אשר אמר ישעיה מוציא כלי למעשיהו.

[[ ]] ונדיבי העמ המה הם הבאים לכרות את הבאר במחוקקות אשר חקק

המחוקק לחת הלך במה בכל קץ הרשיע וזולתם לא ישיגו עד עמד יורה

הצדק באחרית הימים.[[ ]] [[ ]] וכל אשר הובאו בברית...

The Staff is the Interpreter of the Law of whom Isaiah said, 'He makes a tool for His work; and the nobles of the people are those who dug the *Well* with staffs with which the Staff ordained that they should walk in all the age of wickedness—and without them they shall find nothing—until he comes who shall teach righteousness at the end of days...[28]

This text has some textual harmony with Isa 2:1-3 and 26:8. For example, first, the phrase באחרית הימים appears in 2:1 and here in the above text. Secondly, verbal harmony can also be identified as the verbs הלך (to walk) and ירה (to teach) occurs in Isa 2:3 and in the above text. Thirdly there is a reference to תורה (the Law or instruction). In CD 6:4 there is reference to the *Well* which indicates Torah (הבאר היא התורות)—The Well is the Torah which is also

---

[28] Vermes, *The Complete Dead Sea Scrolls in English*, 133.

mentioned in Isa. 2:3 and 26:8. This shows that there is some conceptual harmony between the texts. This conceptual harmony has to do with the "Messianic Teacher at the end of the days" and the Torah.

Regarding referent/s of 'they,' there are no consensus in the scholarship regarding the identity of 'they.' There are scholars who identify המחוקק (the Staff) as the דורש התורה (Interpreter of the Law) is the same figure who comes at the end of days i.e., יורה הצדק (Righteous Teacher).[29] On the other hand, there are others who do not identify these two figures to be the same.[30] In that a clear distinction was made between these two figures. This is to say "Interpreter of the Law" is the historical teacher and "Righteous Teacher" at the end of days is the eschatological teacher.[31] P. R. Davies counters this argument saying that historical teacher has some messianic significance on par with the one who comes at the end of days (CD 6:11).[32] Conversely, Michael Knibb understands "Interpreter of the Law" of the past as an eschatological title for the "Branch of David at the end of days."[33] Moreover this title attested in 4QFlor which is parallel to CD.[34]

---

[29] Robert B Laurin, "Problem of Two Messiahs in the Qumran Scrolls," *RevQ* 4.1 (1963): 49–50; J. M. Allegro, "Further Messianic References in Qumran Literature," *JBL* 75.3 (1956): 176.

[30] M. Black, "Theological Conceptions in the Dead Sea Scrolls," *Exegetisk Arsbok*.18–19 (1953): 86.

[31] Collins, *The Scepter and the Star*, 112.

[32] Philip R Davies, *The Damascus Covenant: An Interpretation of the "Damascus Document"* (JSOTSup 25; Sheffield: JSOT Pr, 1982), 124.

[33] Michael A Knibb, "The Teacher of Righteousness - a Messianic Title," in *A Tribute to Geza Vermes: Essays on Jewish and Christian Literature and History* (Sheffield, Eng: JSOT Pr, 1990), 51–65.

[34] Brooke, *Exegesis at Qumran*, 206–9.

Another issue with the identity of 'they' here is regarding "Messiah of Aaron and Israel." Samuel Raj notes that many scholars agree that Zadokite Messiah of CD is "Messiah of Aaron and Israel."[35] For example, J. T. Milik points out that "Interpreter of the Law" is the "Messiah of Aaron and the High Priest."[36] Similarly, J. Liver finds correspondence between the "Interpreter of the Law" (CD 7:19-20) and "the Branch of David at the end of Days" (4QFlor 1:11-13).[37] In that "Interpreter of the Law" has the same messianic status as that of "the Branch of David" and may be anointed of Aaron at the end of Days. On the other hand, the title "Messiah of Aaron and David" represents both the priestly and the lay aspect of the community. For instance, Schechter thinks that the title "Messiah of Aaron and Israel" is indicative of the lay and priestly dimension of the community.[38] Moreover, he is the first one to identify this title with "Teacher of Righteousness." Conversely, the "Messianic Teacher" would be coming again at the "end of days" (CD 6:11).[39] This may probably be right as there is a reference to the arising of the Teacher of Righteousness with the Messiah of Aaron and Israel (CD 20:1) who would teach the Law.

---

[35] Samuel Raj, *The "Anointed Ones" in the Qumran Literature*, 36.

[36] J. T. Milik as cited by Samuel Raj, *The "Anointed Ones" in the Qumran Literature*, 32.

[37] Jacob Liver, "The Doctrine of the Two Messiahs in Sectarian Literature in the Time of the Second Commonwealth," *HTR* 52.3 (1959): 160–61.

[38] Solomon Schechter cited by Samuel Raj, *The "Anointed Ones" in the Qumran Literature*, 36.

[39] If Schechter's argument is accepted here, then "Teacher of Righteousness" would be great importance to the Christian concepts of incarnation and resurrection in the sect.

Whatever the case may be whether the "Interpreter of the Law" is associated with the "Teacher of Righteousness" and "Messiah of Aaron and Israel," it seems there is some sort of fluidity in the usage of these titles. Collins rightly notes that "This usage suggests that such titles as Interpreter of the Law" and Teacher of Righteousness could be variously used to refer to figures of past or future and they are interchangeable."[40] Moreover, "they" may also represent the community of "Messiah of Aaron and Israel." In that the community of CD saw themselves as "instructors of the Law." Accordingly, Swarup notes that the conglomeration of Zion and Temple motifs, and the scribal change on the ירה (to teach) to mean וירונו (they will teach) for MT's וירונו (he will teach) points to the self-understanding of the community as the "instructors of the Law".[41] If the argument of Collins and Swarup are accepted then the "they" may be "Messiah of Aaron and Israel" which refers to the self-understanding of CD community as "Messianic Teachers"—Interpreter of the Law and also Teacher of Righteousness at the end of days.

Self-understanding of Community as Messianic

The unique readings at Isa 4:2; 11:4; and 61:3 indicate a self-understanding of the community as Messianic. There are three distinct but interrelated ideas that have to do with DSS community's consciousness as messianic. First unique reading at 4:2 indicates צמח (branch) as a messianic title of an individual and also as "root of planting." Secondly, unique

---

[40] Collins, *The Scepter and the Star*, 112.

[41] Swarup, *The Self-Understanding of the Dead Sea Scrolls Community*, 191.

reading at 11:4 has to do with חטר/צמח in relation to the land. Thirdly, the unique reading at 61:3 reflects the corporate idea of community as messianic. The above of distinct ideas of the Scroll were well attested in the Qumran literature.

The unique reading at 4:2 resonates with 4QFlor 3:10-13 (cf. 2 Sam 7:13b-14a; 1QHa 14:14b-15; 16:5b-11). The text of 4QFlor 3:10-11 says:

יל היהי אוהו באל אול היהא ינא סל [לעו] ותכלממ אסכ תא יתוניכהו

הרותה שרוד סע דמיעה דיוד חמצ האוה .ןבל

And the Throne of the Kingdom, I will establish forever. I will be to him as father and he will to me as a son. He is the **branch of David** who will stand with the Interpreter of the Law.

Scroll Isaiah 4:2

והכינותי את כסא ממלכתו [לעו] לם אני אהיה לוא לאב והוא

יהיה לי לבן. הואה צמח דויד העימד עם דורש התורה

On that day the **branch of the LORD** shall be beautiful and glorious, and the fruit of the land shall be pride and glory of the survivors of Israel *and Judah*.

Clearly the word צמח appears in the above texts. 4QFl 3:10-12 is a quotation from 2 Sam 7:13b-14a. In 4QFl 3:12, מח דויד (Branch of David) is the one that God raises at the אחרית הימים (end of days). The verse says קימותי את סוכת דויד ננופלת (I will raise up the **booth of David** which was fallen) which clearly talks about the restoration of Israel. Here is a clear association between

סוכת (booth) and צמח דויד (branch of David) which is an example of *gezerah Shavah*.[42] This leads us to think that the focus of 4QFlor is not on the role of Messiah *per se* but on the self-understanding of the community.[43] Furthermore, the word משיחו (his anointed) in Ps 2:2 appears in 4QFlor 3:19 parallel to the phrase "בחירי ישראל" (the elect of Israel). In that the "elect of Israel" has messianic significance. In fact, the term "משיח" in Qumran literature is rendered to a person or persons with a particular task in the end of days or latter days.[44] Consequently, there is a link between the "elect of Israel" and the anointing. Conversely, Swarup points out to the similar phenomenon regarding the word נצר (shoot) as collective identity of the community in Hodayot document (1QH) (cf. Isa 11:1, 14:19, 60:21, 1QH 14:14b-15; 16:5b-11).[45] So, the word נצר in 4QFlor combines these two aspects— the elect and the anointing of the same. Therefore, it can be assumed that the unique reading at Isa 4:2 resonates with 4QFlor and also with 1QH in which the self-understanding of the community as messianic is very evident.[46]

The second unique reading at 11:4 reflects the idea of "land" and its relationship with צמח דויד (Branch of David.

---

[42] *Gezera Shawa* is Jewish Hermeneutical technique in which two or more words are juxtaposed based on one "catchword" or root shared by them, see, Pulikottil, *Transmission of Biblical Texts in Qumran The Case of the Large Isaiah Scroll 1QISaa*, 74; Brooke, *Exegesis at Qumran*, 23.

[43] Swarup, *The Self-Understanding of the Dead Sea Scrolls Community*, 127.

[44] Brooke, *Exegesis at Qumran*, 197.

[45] Swarup, *The Self-Understanding of the Dead Sea Scrolls Community*, 44, 127.

[46] Swarup, *The Self-Understanding of the Dead Sea Scrolls Community*, 131.

Conceptually, this unique reading reflects 4Q161 (4QPIsa[a]) 3:17-21a which is an interpretation of Isa 11:1-4.

4Q161 3:17-21a (4QPIsa[a]):

פשרו על צמח] דויד העומד באח[רית הימים] אויבו ואל יסומכנו

ב[...ה] תורה כסא לבוד נזר ק[ודש] ובגדי רוקמו[ת...]

בידו ובכול הג[ראי]ם ימשול ומגוג [...] העמים תשפוט הרבו

The [interpretation concerning the **shoot**] of David who will stand in the e[nd of days…], his enemies and God will uphold him with […the] Law […t]hrone; of glory, a ho[ly] crown, and garments of variegate[ed stuff…] in his hands, and over all the na[tions] be shall rule, and Magog, [all] the people he shall judge by his sword.[47]

Pesher here interprets Isa 11:1-4 with reference to **Shoot of David** (צמח דויד) as a triumphant individual who comes at the end of time and who God sustains with His Spirit to rule over the nations and judge them. This same interpretation is echoed in Isaiah's חטר ישי (**Shoot of Jesse**) in 11:1.[48] In that the unique reading of the Scroll follows royal messianic tradition in which the Shoot would come from Davidic line. However, Swarup observes a progression of development in the messianic tradition.[49] In that the ideal of eschatological royal figure has been reworked in Isa 60:2 and 55:3. In 60:2

---

[47] John M Allegro, ed., *DJD V: Qumrân Cave 4* (Oxford: Clarendon Pr, 1968), 14.

[48] This word occurs in 4QPIsaa 8:11 and also in 4Q285 5:2 parallel to נצר (branch), see, David J. A. Clines, ed., *DCH VIII* ת־ש: 202.

[49] Swarup, *The Self-Understanding of the Dead Sea Scrolls Community*, 45.

the focus is on the land and in 55:3 the focus in on the community. Clearly the focus is shifted from an individual to the community and the land. For instance Otto Eissfeldt argues that in Isa 55:1-5, the covenant made with David applies to people of Israel as well.[50] Vermes understands this **"Branch of David"** as the "Prince of Congregation" who is the messiah—the shoot of Jesse. His main function is to judge, smite the *earth/land,* and kills the wicked (cf. Isa 11:4).[51] On the other hand, Collins notes that in relation to Isa 11, 4Q285 War Scroll understand the **Shoot of Jesse** having messianic function of judging, striking the land/earth and kill the wicked.[52] So, the title "Prince of Congregation" is well attested in CD (CD 7:20), and 1QM (5:1). So, if this exegetical context of the CD and 1QM is taken into consideration and also unique reading 4:2, then the **Branch of David**—an eschatological figure who would rule the land with justice. In that the community itself should appropriate such an ideal until the eschatological figure comes and leads them further.

The third unique reading at 61:3 appropriated messianic ideal in the understanding of community as "remnant." Swarup notes that Isa 61:3 reflects an idea of remnant that is undergirded corporate consciousness of the community as "eternal plant-righteous remnant."[53] This is the transfer

---

[50] Otto Eissfeldt, "Promises of Grace to David in Isaiah 55:1-5," in *Israel's Prophetic Heritage; Essays in Honor of James Muilenburg* (Harper, 1962), 206-7.

[51] Géza Vermès, "The Oxford Forum for Qumran Research: Seminar on the Rule of War from Cave 4 (4Q285)," *JJS* 43.1 (1992): 88.

[52] Collins, *The Scepter and the Star*, 65.

[53] Swarup, *The Self-Understanding of the Dead Sea Scrolls Community*, 21.

of idea from factuality of 'no-temple' to conceptuality of "elect/remnant".[54] In that מטע יהוה (planting of the LORD) refers to the whole of Israel who will be righteous and inherit the land forever. Swarup suggests that this aspect has been appropriated by the DSS community for themselves.[55] For instance this aspect is reflected in CD 12:22:

הזה יתהלכו זרע ישראל ולא יוארו

That **Seed of Israel** shall continue to walk and they shall not be cursed.

Talmon notes that the Yaḥad members saw themselves as true זרע ישראל (Seed of Israel) in CD 12:21-22 who is זרע קדש (Holy Seed) in Isa. 6:3.[56] This holy seed is favored by God to fill the whole land (CD 2:11-12) forever (1QH 17:14).[57] This Holy Seed is מטע יהוה (planting of the LORD), and the זרע ישראל (Seed of Israel). This self-understanding of the community, according to Dimant is a sectarian understanding of the Elect and Just.[58] Moreover, Collins notes that the **Shoot** in 1QHª 16:10 associated with Suffering Servant of Isa 53:3.[59]

---

[54] Shemaryahu Talmon, "The Internal Diversification of Judaism in the Early Second Temple Period," in *Jewish Civilization in the Hellenistic-Roman Period* (Sheffield, England: JSOT Pr, 1991), 22–23.

[55] Swarup, *The Self-Understanding of the Dead Sea Scrolls Community*, 23.

[56] Shemaryahu Talmon, "Waiting for the Messiah at Qumran," in *Judaisms and Their Messiahs at the Turn of the Christian Era* (eds. Jacob Neusner, W. S. Green, and E. S. Frerichs; Cambridge, England: Cambridge Univ Pr, 1987), 117.

[57] Talmon, "Waiting for the Messiah at Qumran," 117.

[58] Dimant as cited by, Swarup, *The Self-Understanding of the Dead Sea Scrolls Community*, 24.

[59] Collins, *The Scepter and the Star*, 146.

Similarly, Swarup points out to "Holy Seed" in 1QHᵃ 16:10-11 have some allusions to the one of the Servant songs (cf. Isa 53:3b).[60]

1QHᵃ 16:10-11:

ומפרית נצר ק[ו]דש למטעת אמת סותר

בלוא נחשב. ובלא נודע חותם רזו

And the bud (Shoot) of holiness of the plant of truth was hidden and was not esteemed, and being unperceived, its mystery was sealed.[61]

Isa 53:3b

וּכְמַסְתֵּר פָּנִים מִמֶּנּוּ נִבְזֶה וְלֹא חֲשַׁבְנֻהוּ

And as one from whom other hide their faces, he was despised, and we held him of no account (not esteemed)

Textual harmony between the roots סתר√ and חשב√ can be identified. This shows that the scribe of 1QHᵃ might have alluded his hymn at 1QHᵃ 16:10-11 with Isa. 53:3b especially in relation to "hidden" (סתר√) and "esteem" (חשב√). However, 1QHᵃ applies שדוק רצנ (Holy Seed) to whole community. In that the hymn has reworked the understanding of suffering servant of Isaiah to appropriate the same to whole community.[62] Clearly, this means that community saw themselves as messianic. In that they saw

---

[60] Swarup, *The Self-Understanding of the Dead Sea Scrolls Community*, 47.

[61] Vermes, *The Complete Dead Sea Scrolls in English*, 284.

[62] Swarup, *The Self-Understanding of the Dead Sea Scrolls Community*, 47.

themselves as appropriating the role of the 'Servant' who is a messianic figure.

Messiah as Son of God

The unique readings at Isa 7:14 and Isa 9:5-6 are indicative of the messianic idea of the Scroll regarding the Son of Man. The unique reading at 7:14 reflects the idea of christening of Messiah by God. It also reflects the idea of "begetting Messiah." The unique reading at 9:5-6 talks about the "peace" that Messiah would bring in. In that Son of Man may also be regarded as "Herald of peace."

The idea of God christening his Messiah at 7:14 is quite unique to the Scroll only. This was not attested anywhere in the Qumran scrolls. However, the concept of "begetting messiah" appears in the Rule of the Congregation (1QSa 2:11-12) which says

1QSa 2:11-12:

[ה מו]שב אנשי השם [קריאי] מועד לעצת היחד אם יולד. [אל]

א]ת[המשיח אתם יבוא [הכוהן] רואש. כול עדת ישראל

[This shall be ass]embly of the men of renown called to the meeting of the council of the community. When God engenders (the Priest-) Messiah, he shall come with them [at] the head of the whole congregation of Israel…[63]

---

[63] Vermes, *The Complete Dead Sea Scrolls in English*, 161.

There is an issue with the word יוליד (Hiph Imperfect third masculine singular √ילד 'to beget a child') in the text. Barthelemy initially reads this blurred word as "יוליד" with אל as the subject of the verb to mean "when God begets Messiah..."[64] However, later he adopts J. T. Milik's proposal to read it as "יוליך" to mean "When God shall lead..."[65] However Robert Gordis rejects this emendation on the basis of Hebrew syntax of the text that reflects regular Hebrew usage of verb followed by the subject.[66] So, there he does not see any logical inconsistency in the syntax and hence no reason to change verb from יוליד (to beget) to יוליך (to lead). On the other hand, Dupont-Sommer while reconstructing this text with אדני (Lord) in the place of אל, suggests that this text has allusions to Ps 2:7.[67] In that he understands, the "begotten son" in our text in the light of Ps. 2:7 as "Son of God."[68] Samuel Raj, on the contrary, accepts Milik's emendation keeping in mind easily confused words in the Qumran scrolls such as *yod* and *waw* and *daleth* and *kaph*.[69] However, it is not wise to rule out the possibility of reading יוליד (to beget) rendering it as a scribal error caused out of confusion of letters. In fact, Frank M. Cross asserts that the contended word יוליד certainly

---

[64] Dominique Barthélemy and Jozef Tadeusz Milik, DJD I: *Qumran Cave 1* (Oxford: Clarendon, 1955), 110.

[65] Barthélemy and Milik, *DJD I*: 117.

[66] Robert Gordis, "'Begotten' Messiah in the Qumran Scrolls," *VT* 7.2 (1957): 192.

[67] André Dupont-Sommer, *The Essene Writings from Qumran*, Meridian Books (Cleveland: World Pub, 1962), 108.

[68] Dupont-Sommer, *The Essene Writings from Qumran*, 108.

[69] Samuel Raj, *The "Anointed Ones" in the Qumran Literature*, 66.

is the correct word based on the newly infra-red plates.[70] Moreover, the idea of God begetting is very much present in the Biblical traditions as it has allusions to the same in Ps 2:7 and Isa 66:9.[71] Furthermore, Gracías Martínez in light of 11QMelchizedek and 1QM suggests that the "Son of Man" in 4Q246 as "Melchizedek, Michael or the Prince of light."[72] Moreover, the concept of divine begetting is very much part of OT tradition. For example, Brandon Crowe argues that filial imagery can be observed in the Song of Moses (Deut 32:1-43).[73] He further notes that the verb ילד (to beget) is used in Deut 32:18 which indicate a "rare language of God begetting of Israel."[74] In addition to this, L. Novakovic points to Matthew's use of the verb γεννάω (to beget) in Matt 1:20 allude to aspect of God begetting Messiah.[75] The Greek verb γεννάω that occurs in Ps 2:7 is alluded in 1QSa 2:11. Therefore, Milik's emendation to read יוליד may not be plausible at

---

[70] Frank Moore Cross, "Qumran Cave I," *JBL* 5.2 (1956): 124–25.

[71] Cross, "Qumran Cave I," 124.

[72] Florentino García Martínez, "Two Messianic Figures in the Qumran Texts," in *Current Research and Technological Developments on the Dead Sea Scrolls: Conference on the Texts from the Judean Desert, Jerusalem, 30 April 1995* (Leiden: E J Brill, 1996), 20–24.

[73] Brandon D Crowe, "The Song of Moses and Divine Begetting in Matt 1,20," *Bib* 90.1 (2009): 48.

[74] The Song of Moses is well attested in 4QDeut^c, 4QPaleoDeut^r and in non-biblical scrolls like CD 5:16-17, 1QS 9:23, 1QM 12:11-12, and 1QH XIII 10.27. Moreover the √ילד occur in MT of Num 11:12 and Ps 2:7 which is parallel to 1QSa 2:11, see, Crowe, "The Song of Moses and Divine Begetting in Matt 1, 20," 43, 48, and 50.

[75] Lidija Novakovic, *Messiah, the Healer of the Sick: A Study of Jesus as the Son of David in the Gospel of Matthew* (WMANT; Tübingen: Mohr Siebeck, 2003), 22.

1QSa 2:11. Therefore, the Scroll's idea of God christening his Messiah by naming him indicates the legitimization of Messiah as the Son of God who God begot. This idea resonates well with 1QSa and other Qumran writings as mentioned above.

The unique readings at Isa 9:5-6 reflects the idea of Peace and the messianic figure—the Herald of Peace. The explicative addition of article on שלום (Peace) at Isa 9:5 resonates with 11QMelch 2:15-16

הזואת הואה יום ה[שלום א]שר...ביד ישע[יה הנביא אשר [מה] נאור

על הרים רגל[י] מבש[ר מ]שמיע שלום מבנשר

טוב משמיע ישוע[ה [א]ומר לציון [מלד] אלוהיך

This is the day of [peace/salvation] concerning which [God] spoke [through Isa]iah the prophet, who said [how] beautiful upon the mountains are the feet of the Herald[76] who proclaims peace who brings good news, who proclaims salvation, who says to Zion, "Your God [reigns]…"[77]

The idea of "the day of peace" here in the above text resonates with Isa 52:7 (cf. unique reading 9:5). On the other hand, the verb בשר "to preach good news" on the day of שלום (Peace) seems to be the function of the Herald. The identity of the Herald is indicated as "the one who is anointed" in 11QMelch 2:18. He is anointed of the Spirit as mentioned in Daniel 9:25—משיח הרוח [הו]אה]—[the one an]ointed of the Spir[it] about] (cf. 11QMelch 2:18). He is a prophetic figure in CD 2:12 as the phrase משיח הרוח (anointed of the

____

[76] As translated by Collins, *The Scepter and the Star*, 133.

[77] Vermes, *The Complete Dead Sea Scrolls in English*, 533.

Spirit) occurs.[78] In addition to this, the unique reading at 9:6 focuses on Messianic child. This verse has some textual harmony with Ps 2:7-8 and 4QFl 3:10-13. This verse is also a quotation from 2 Sam 7:14. The reference to צמח דויד (Branch of David) is an indicative of Messianic child is the Herald of Peace and also the Davidic Messiah. He is also the Son of God. Collins makes a very interesting observation regarding above. According to him, "The citation from 2 Sam 7 provides an explicit basis for identifying the Branch of David as the Son of God. Since the Branch is explicitly called Messiah of Righteousness in the Patriarchal Blessings (4Q252=4QPGen), it is surely justified to speak of him as Davidic Messiah."[79] Therefore, the unique readings at 9:5-6 reflect the idea of the day of Peace and the Herald of Peace which resonates with 11QMelch, and CD.

Messianic Age

The unique reading 11:9 (cf. 2:3) reflects the futuristic reading in the Scroll and is indicative of the "messianic age" which resonates with the Qumran understanding of אחרית הימים (end of days). Talmon suggests that Qumran covenanters understood "age to come" as part of the actual history and expected a 'preordained' stage to set in.[80] Conversely, he understood this "age to come" as Messianic age that has real historical character.[81] On the other hand, Philip R. Davies indicates that the Qumran community saw themselves as

---

⁷⁸ Collins, *The Scepter and the Star*, 134.

⁷⁹ Collins, *The Scepter and the Star,* 185.

⁸⁰ Talmon, "Waiting for the Messiah at Qumran," 128.

⁸¹ Talmon, "Waiting for the Messiah at Qumran," 126.

"bridging" the gap between this age and the age to come.[82] This idea resonates with the unique reading at Isa 4:2 which was dealt above (cf. Self-understanding of Community as Messianic; 4Q161 3:17). The phrase "end of days" occurs in CD 4:4 that mention "Sons of Zadok" as "elect of Israel, the men called by name who (shall) stand at the end of days." The verb עמד in CD 4:4 occurs in CD 6:11; 7:20; and 4QFl 1:11. In CD 6:11, the verb occurs in relation to the messianic figure who would teach righteousness. In CD 7:20, it occurs in relation to the Prince of the Congregation. In 4QFlor 1:11, it occurs in relation to the Branch of David who will arise at the end of days with the Interpreter of the Law. Collins notes that these texts refer to a future event.[83] On the contrary, Brooke suggests that the future time is in the process of realizing and that the later days are not the end of days but they inaugurate the same.[84] Wise argues against this suggestion and indicates that the "end of days" is a first stage in two-stage eschatology.[85] Therefore, looking at the occurrence of this phrase in relation to the messianic figures in the above Qumran writings, messianic age may be considered as "age to come." Annette Steudel rightly says that the phrase may refer to past, present, and future but messianic references are futuristic.[86] Therefore, messianic age is part of end of days which is proleptic in nature.

---

[82] Philip R Davies, "Eschatology at Qumran," *JBL* 104.1 (1985): 39.

[83] Collins, *The Scepter and the Star*, 114–15.

[84] Brooke, *Exegesis at Qumran*, 176.

[85] Michael O Wise, "4QFlorilegium and the Temple of Adam," *RevQ* 15.1–2 (1991): 115.

[86] Annette Steudel as cited by, Collins, *The Scepter and the Star,* 115.

יחד *as Messianic Community*

The unique readings at Isa 40:5 and 50:8 reflect יחד community consciousness as messianic.[87] The Yaḥad community saw themselves as community in waiting until the Messiah of Aaron and Israel arise. For example, 1QS 9:10-11; CD 12:22-23; 19:34-20:1; and 14:18-19 point to the יחד in waiting until the Messiah of Aaron and Israel arise.[88] Moreover Isa 40:8 speak of anticipation for the revelation of God in the future and 50:8 speaks of Servant's vindication that anticipates restoration of Israel. This aspect of revelation and restoration corresponds to the "wilderness theology" of the Yaḥad community. In that the wilderness is the place of revelation and restoration takes place (1QS 5:6-7; 8:1-16a; 9:3-11).[89] Moreover, Yaḥad's self-understanding as "Temple of Men" in contrast to the Temple of Israel of the past and in anticipation of "Temple of Yahweh" in the future is indicative of their "interim" character as Messianic community.[90] Pulikottil rightly suggested that the self-understanding of Yaḥad as "Temple of Men" (present reality) is an "interim" stage between "Temple of Israel" (past) and "Temple of Yahweh" (Age to come).[91] So, one finds here a congruence of past,

---

[87] Cf. Isa 41:1, 20, 23; 43:9, 17; 45:16, 21; 46:2; 48:13; 52:8, 9; 60:13; 66:17.

[88] Talmon, "The Concept of Māšîah and Messianism in Early Judaism," 105.

[89] Alison Schofield, *From Qumran to the Yaḥad: A New Paradigm of Textual Development for The Community Rule* (STDJ 77; Leiden: Brill, 2009), 278.

[90] It is already noted at unique reading 2:3 where the omission of the phrase אל הר יהוה (to the mountain of the LORD) and the change in person in the verb to וירונו (and they will teach) suggests the relocation of Torah and settlement to Qumran., see, Pulikottil, *Transmission of Biblical Texts*, 173.

[91] Pulikottil, *Transmission of Biblical Texts*, 174.

present and future in the Yaḥad community. In that Yaḥad Messianism can be seen as "unrealized Messianism" which will be fully consummated by the coming of Messiahs at the "turn of events" (end of days).[92] In addition to this, the unique reading at 50:8 where the scribe changed MT's יחד to יחדין is indicative of יחד as collective representation of עבד יהוה (the Servant of the LORD). Swarup rightly suggests that the notion of Messiah not only applied to the Messiahs but also to the whole community.[93] Therefore, the notion of Messiah not only projected to the eschatological figures but also to the community at large 'waiting' and preparing for the coming of the Messiahs.

Messianic Servant

The unique readings at 42:1; 49:2, 6; 50:4; 52:14; 61:1 and 62:11 reflect a particular understanding of the Scroll in relation to עבד־יהוה (the Servant of the LORD) which has some conceptual affinities with Qumran understanding. First, unique reading at 42:1 is indicative of "heightened authority" of the Servant. The addition of 3ms Ps is suggestive of the same. Chamberlain notes that in the Scroll the ethical qualities are often understood as descriptive names for Messiah.[94] If Chamberlain's view is correct then 42:1 points to legal and judicial role of Messianic Servant which was delegated by

---

[92] Talmon, "The Concept of Māšîah and Messianism in Early Judaism," 109.

[93] Swarup, *The Self-Understanding of the Dead Sea Scrolls Community*, 49.

[94] Chamberlain, "Functions of God as Messianic Titles in the Complete Qumran Isaiah Scroll," 369.

YHWH. For example, 42:1 has some conceptual affinity with 1QH[a] 15:6-7 which says,

אודלה אדוני כי סמכתני בעוזכה ורוח

קוד שכה הניפותה בי בל אמוט

I thank, Oh Lord! For you have *upheld* me by your might and have poured out your Holy Spirit within me, and you have extended to be, never I will be shaken.[95]

Clearly the above text has conceptual affinities with 42:1 (cf. 61:1) where it talks about endowment of the Servant with the Spirit. Especially, 61:1 talks specifically about function of the Servant. For example, 1QH[a] 23:14 echoes the understanding of 61:1 in which the mission of the Servant is described.

On the other hand, the unique reading at 49:2 project prophetic function of the Servant which has conceptual affinity with some Qumran texts. Goldingay and Payne understand the preposition "כְּ" here as indicative of identity of the Servant.[96] For instance, פי (mouth) is usually considered as prophets' tool of acting.[97] This is indicative of prophet's role to teach the community. So, if the Servant is the prophet with a teaching function, then who is this figure in the Qumran literature? For instance, in the earlier scholarship, the Teacher is indentified as "prophet like Moses" envisaged in Deut 18: 18-19 quoted

---

[95] Collins, *The Scepter and the Star*, 147.

[96] Goldingay and Payne, *Isaiah 40-55*, vo.1, 157.

[97] Goldingay and Payne, *Isaiah 40-55*, vol. 1, 155.

in 4QT (4Q175) 5-8 and in 1QS 9.⁹⁸ These passages present us with some difficulties. Collins notes that these passages imply that the eschatological prophet who would teach has already arrived but it is not so in CD 6 which is similar to 1QS 9.⁹⁹ However, much stronger case can be made with CD 6:11 which is influenced by Deut 18:18 and Hos 10:12. As noted above Deut 18:18 is cited in 4Q175 5-8 (4QT) which says,

נבי אקים לאהמה מקרב אחיהמה כמוכה ונתתי דברי בפיהו וידבר
אליהמה אי לול אשר אצוונו. והיה האיש אשר לוא
ישמעאל דברי אשר ידבר הנבי בשמי אנוכי אדרוש מעמו

Prophet like you I will raise up from among their brethren. I will put my words into his mouth, and he shall tell them all that I have commanded him. And I will require a reckoning whoever does not listen to the words which the prophet shall speak in my name.¹⁰⁰

Clearly the above passage has allusions with Deut 18:18 and Hos 10:12.¹⁰¹ This vividly shows that 1QS and 4QT expected the prophet at the end of the days who would teach the law to the community. Whether or not this prophet figure comes before or after the "anointed ones" but it seems his function to teach very much reflects the messianic figures—

---

⁹⁸ Vermes, *The Complete Dead Sea Scrolls in English*, 185–86; Michael O Wise, "The Temple Scroll and the Teacher of Righteousness," in *Mogilany 1989: Papers on the Dead Sea Scrolls Offered in Memory of Jean Carmignac* (Cracow: Enigma Pr, 1993), 142.

⁹⁹ Collins, *The Scepter and the Star*, 124.

¹⁰⁰ Vermes, *The Complete Dead Sea Scrolls in English*, 527.

¹⁰¹ Later Jewish traditions associated the Teacher with Elijah, see, J. Jermias, "Ηλ(ε)Ιας," ed. Gerhard Kittel, *TDNT* II: 932.

Teacher of Righteousness and the Interpreter of the Law.[102] The same idea is reflected in Isa 49:2 where the teaching function of the prophet is reflected upon the עבד־יהוה. In that case, the prophet in 1QS and 4QT is a forerunner of the eschatological messianic figures.[103] It follows that the teaching function of this prophetic figure will be fully appropriated by the Messianic figures of the end of days. Therefore, the same expectation is reflected on the Servant of the LORD in the Scroll in 49:2.

Similarly, the unique reading at 50:4 reflects the same idea of 49:2. However, there is an additional aspect of the Servant being a 'student' of YHWH. In that the Servant will be taught by God so that he could teach. This idea is well attested in 1QH[a] 15:10 which says,

ואתה אלי נתת <נ> י לעפים לעצת קובש

ות[למדני] בברית כה ולשוני כלמידיד

You O LORD! You have placed me among the branches of the council of holiness, and you have taught my tongue by your covenant and according to your teaching.

There is a clear conceptual and textual affinity between 50:4 and the above text. Swarup finds textual affinity between 50:4 and 1QH XVI (VIII):36 and finds that the Psalmist of 1QH appropriated the role of the servant in Isa 50:4.[104] Conversely, Michael O. Wise finds lot of allusions of Servant Songs in the Hodayot.[105] For instance like Servant, the Teacher also is

---

[102] Samuel Raj, *The "Anointed Ones" in the Qumran Literature*, 47.

[103] Samuel Raj, *The "Anointed Ones" in the Qumran Literature*, 42.

[104] Swarup, *The Self-Understanding of the Dead Sea Scrolls Community*, 48.

[105] Wise, *The First Messiah*, 290.

endowed by the Spirit and has a 'disciples 'tongue.'[106] Moreover, this 'disciples' tongue' becomes a distinguishing factor not only of the Servant but to the whole community. William M. Schniedewind rightly points to a sectarian language ideology that is reflected in Isa 50:4 which is alluded conceptually in the above text.[107] Therefore, the Teacher may be seeing himself as the Servant in an allusive manner.

The unique readings at 52:14; 61:1 and 62:11 project an idea of "anointing" of the Servant which is echoed in the Qumran literature.[108] For instance, Isa 52:14 talks about vicarious suffering of the Servant where as 61:1 and 62:11 has to do with "anointing" by the Spirit to fulfill the mission that was entrusted to the Servant. There is no consensus regarding the idea of vicarious suffering of the Servant in the Qumran literature. One camp finds evidence for the Suffering Messiah in pre-Christian Judaism whereas the other does not see any reference to the suffering Messiah in the pre-Christian Judaism. For instance A. Dupont-Sommer caused a sensation in the scholarship in 1950 when he suggested that the Teacher of Righteousness is the Suffering Messiah in Deutero-Isaiah.[109] He notes that 52:14 reflects the Sect's belief that "highest embodiment of the Servant of the LORD

---

[106] Collins, *The Scepter and the Star*, 147.

[107] William M Schniedewind, "Qumran Hebrew as an Antilanguage," *JBL.* 118.2 (1999): 240.

[108] Already it is noted that this passage is line with the popular Jewish Messianism., see, Pulikottil, *Transmission of Biblical Texts*, 153.

[109] A. Dupont-Sommer as cited by, Brownlee, "The Servant of the LORD in the Qumran Scrolls I," 9.

would be in Messiah."[110] So, the 'anointing' of the Servant is utmost important for the Sect. Conversely, Barthélemy prefers the word "anointed" for marred for three reasons. They are: first, 52:14 has grammatical allusion to Ps 45:8. Secondly, the word 'anoint' is syntactically appropriate as it does not cause any syntactical problem. Thirdly, it avoids *hapax legomenon*.[111] Similarly more recently Collins pointed out that in the Targum the messianic passages Isa 52 and 53 were "systematically" modified to avoid the interpretation that the Servant has to suffer.[112] However, Jean Starcky observes the notion of Suffering Servant in 4Q541 (4QAaron A).[113] Similarly, Émile Peuch agrees with Starcky.[114] However this text does not correlate with the Suffering of the Servant of the LORD. Nevertheless, the trials described in 4Q541 correlates with the trials of the Teacher of Righteousness in CD 1. Therefore, the unique reading at 52:14 reflects the primacy of the idea of 'anointing' of the Servant which is shared by other Qumran literature.

The unique reading at 61:1 talks about the task of the Servant who is "anointed." The addition of *waw* as noted

---

[110] Brownlee, "The Servant of the LORD in the Qumran Scrolls I," 10.

[111] Brownlee, "The Servant of the LORD in the Qumran Scrolls I," 10 .

[112] Collins, *The Scepter and the Star*, 143.

[113] Jean Starcky, "Les Quatre Étapes Du Messianisme à Qumran," *RB* 70.4 (1963): 492, as cited by Collins, *The Scepter and the Star*, 142.

[114] Émile Puech, "Fragments d'un Apocryphe de Lévi et Le Personnage Eschatologique: 4QTestLévic-d(?) Et 4QAJa," in *The Madrid Qumran Congress: Proceedings of the International Congress on the Dead Sea Scrolls, Madrid, 18-21 March 1991* (Leiden: E J Brill, 1992), 492–99, as cited by Collins, *The Scepter and the Star*, 142.

earlier is for two reasons: punctuation and to make the infinitives dependent on the main verb משח "to anoint." So, there is a link between משח and the tasks of the Servant. These tasks involve בשר (to bring glad tidings) and חבש (to heal). Keeping this in mind, 61:1 has conceptual affinity with 4Q521 (Messianic Apocalypse) fragment ii:2 (cf. Ps 146:6-8). In this text, God is the one who is subject of preaching good news. For example, in v. 12 it says,

כי ירפא חללים ומתים יהיה ענוים יבשר

For He will heal the wounded; give life to the dead and preach the good news to the poor.

There is verbal harmony between 61:1 and the above text. The √בשר occurs in both the texts which reflects the responsibility of the preaching the good news. The former indicates that the Servant is the subject but in the later God is the subject of the verb בשר (to preach glad tidings). The idea of healing is reflected in the verb חבש (to bind up) in 61:1 and the verb רפא "to heal" in 4Q521. Moreover, this text in 4Q521 has allusions to Ps 146:6-8. So, this is clearly a case for verbal and conceptual harmonization. Similar aspect of prophets being anointed is attested in CD 2:12 and 1QM 11:7 where we find the expression "anointed Ones."[115] Furthermore, the verb בשר occurs in 11QMelch 2:15-16 which says

על הרים רגל]י[מבש]ר ס[שמיע שלום מב]שר[
טוב משמיע ישוע]ה [א]ומר לציון]מלך[אלוהיך

---

[115] Collins, *The Scepter and the Star*, 133.

How beautiful on the mountains are the feet of Herald who preaches peace, the Herald of good news, the Herald of salvation who says to Zion, "your God reigns."

In this text מבשר refers to the Herald who proclaims salvation and comforts the mourners of Zion. The aspect of Herald proclaiming salvation is reflected by the unique reading 62:11. This text clearly has textual allusions with Isa 52:7 and 61:1. Therefore, the unique reading at 61:1 emphasizes the importance of anointing in order to perform the tasks of בשר (to bring good news) and חבש (to bind/heal) that is shared by other Qumran literature especially 4Q521 and 11QMelch. The unique reading at 62:11 which reflects the idea of proclaiming salvation resonates with 11QMelch as well.

יחד Messianic Milieu

The Scroll has ideological affinity with other Biblical and Qumran literature in relation to its Messianic expectation. The messianic expectation of the Scroll corresponds more closely with the Yaḥad Messianism. Pulikottil already established that fact that 1QIsaᵃ reflects Yaḥad sensibilities.[116] However, Williamson expresses his doubts whether the Yaḥad documents were used in the Scroll as he finds no evidence for the same.[117] Inversely, R. P. Gordon agrees that there are some ideological concerns of the Scroll that reflect Yaḥad sensibilities.[118] Tov further substantiates this point by

---

[116] Pulikottil, *Transmission of Biblical Texts*, 165–85.

[117] H G M Williamson, "Transmission of Biblical Texts in Qumran: The Case of the Large Isaiah Scroll 1QIsaa," *JTS* 54.2 (2003): 642–43.

[118] Robert P Gordon, "Transmission of Biblical Texts in Qumran: The Case of the Large Isaiah Scroll 1QIsaa," *JSOT* 26.5 (2002): 224.

identifying twenty eight biblical texts written by using QSP.[119] He further notes that the same practice is reflected in CD, 1QHᵃ, 1QM, 1QS, and *Pesharim* which may be called Yaḥad documents.[120] Furthermore, Tov observes that the same practice is reflected in 1QIsaᵃ which is more inclined to 1QS.[121]

Inclination Towards the Rule of Community (1QS)

The Messianism of the Scroll is more inclined to 1QS out of all the Yaḥad documents. For instance, the aspect of "desert/wilderness" and self-understanding of community resonates well with the Scroll's Messianism. Schofield notes that "desert" has a very important place in theology of 1QS community. According to him, "The wilderness was for the Yaḥad a symbolic locale, the site of the greatest covenantal activity at Sinai which the covenanters celebrated annually. There, with their Moses-like Teacher, they describe themselves as if they are Israel *redivivus* encamped in wilderness (Num 1-2; Exod 18:21-22 cf. CD 13:1; 1QS 2:21-22)."[122] This sectarian trait was already noted at unique reading 2:3. Moreover, Pulikottil identifies similar trait in Isa 8:11 in which we find Yaḥad rhetoric, in this case the rhetoric is in 1QSᵃ.[123] Moreover,

---

[119] Tov, *Textual Criticism of the Hebrew Bible*, 104.

[120] Tov, *Textual Criticism of the Hebrew Bible*, 104.

[121] Tov, *Textual Criticism of the Hebrew Bible*, 192.

[122] Schofield, *From Qumran to the Yaḥad*, 269–70.

[123] The Scroll at Isa 8:11 in the second line read יסרני מלכת בדרך העם־הזה (*he turned me from walking in the way of this people*). The issue here is root substitution by the Scribe to read ייסירנו instead of ויסרני. The √סור in the Scroll means to "turn aside" whereas in MT the √יסר means "discipline." Moreover, the same phrase is reflected in 1QSᵃ: ואנשי בריתם אשר ס]רו מלכת בר]רך, see, Pulikottil, *Transmission of Biblical Texts*, 177–78.

Collins notes that the community of 1QS practiced celibacy and more sectarian in nature who lived in Qumran in contrast to the community of CD who lived in villages and towns.[124] Interestingly, Schofield rightly indicates that the sectarian movement is based on "ideological boundaries" which emphasizes on the study of Torah and self-understanding as the community that prepares the way of the LORD (1QS 8:14-16).[125] These ideological boundaries forms "Ipse identity" that issues in the metaphorical representation of the community as "the most holy dwelling" (1QS 8:8), "Covenant" (1QS 1:16 cf. CD 2:2), "Congregation of Israel" (1QS[a] 1:1), and "children of light" (1QM 1:11).[126]

In addition to the above, the themes such as the self-understanding of the community as "the Temple," emphasis of the study of Torah, perfection and holiness are reflected in their messianic expectation. First, as the "Temple of Men" in contrast to the "Temple of Israel" in the past and in anticipation of the "Temple of YHWH" in future, the community devoted

---

[124] Collins notes that the community consists of small quorum of twelve men and three priests who goes into wilderness to prepare the way of the

LORD, see, John J. (John Joseph) Collins, "Beyond the Qumran Community: Social Organization in the Dead Sea Scrolls," *Dead Sea Discov.* 16.3 (2009): 351.

[125] Schofield, *From Qumran to the Yaḥad*, 278.

[126] Ipse Identity means self perception that differentiates the self in contrast to the others. It is personal identity. This has to be understood in the "network of identities." This means that the self-understanding of 1QS community has to understood in the light of the network of identities in the Yaḥad community, see, Jutta Jokiranta, "An Experiment on Idem Identity in the Qumran Movement," *DSD* 16.3 (2009): 312, 315.

themselves in the study of Torah.[127] It was already illustrated the previous section that יחד messianic consciousness is reflected in their self-understanding as the "Temple of Men. Secondly, the emphasis of the study of Torah reflects messianic hope. Pulikottil observes that in Yaḥad literature the enthusiasm to study Torah not only equips them for the later days but also reflects their messianic hope.[128] In that Messiah will be taught by the community before he assumes his messianic role.[129] This idea where the Messiah would be taught by someone is reflected in unique reading 50:4. However, the Scroll here has conceptual affinity with 1QH in which God is the one who teaches Messiah. Nevertheless, the idea of Messiah being taught can be related to the aspect of Yaḥad teaching its messiah. Finally, the concern to be perfect and ethically upright is paramount importance to the community (1QS 8:1-2).[130] This in fact is responsibility of the "Council of the Community" that consists of twelve men and three priests. However, these responsibilities are reflected to the entire community.[131] So as the "Temple of Men" the community is an "interim" stage who are supposed to be doers of Torah until the coming of Messiahs. This idea is reflected in unique readings 40:5 and 50:8. Related to this aspect of perfection and ethical uprightness, holiness is the

---

[127] Collins, "Beyond the Qumran Community," 357; Pulikottil, *Transmission of Biblical Texts*, 175.

[128] Pulikottil, *Transmission of Biblical Texts*, 176.

[129] Pulikottil, *Transmission of Biblical Texts, 176.*

[130] James H Charlesworth, "Community Organization," ed. Lawrence H Schiffman and James C VanderKam, *Encyclopedia of the Dead Sea Scroll* I: 134.

[131] Collins, "Beyond the Qumran Community," 364.

chief end of the community.[132] These ethical ideals are to be appropriated in the messianic age (cf. unique reading 2:3 and 11:9).

Therefore, the messianic milieu of the Scroll may be Yaḥad community. Messianic ideas that are reflected in some of the unique readings shows that the messianic milieu is more inclined towards the sectarian community 1QS than others. However, such an understanding should be anchored in the "network of identities" of Qumran Messianism. In that "network of identities," some ideas are treated as central and some peripheral.[133] Nevertheless, the Scroll while reflecting a common biblical and Qumran Messianism, it displayed its own unique Messianism. This Messianism resonated in the Yaḥad documents but more inclined to 1QS as illustrated above.

Conclusion

This chapter illustrated that the messianic significance of some of the unique readings in the Scroll resonates with Yaḥad documents and in particular 1QS. So, Yaḥad community and in particular 1QS may be messianic milieu of the Scroll. In order to substantiate this, harmonization method which is a part of textual criticism has been followed. This has helped to identify messianic milieu of the Scroll by looking at textual and conceptual affinities. In that first ideological affinities were identified between the Scroll and the other biblical and Qumran literature. Seven ideas were identified which resonates

---

[132] Carol A Newsom, *The Self as Symbolic Space: Constructing Identity and Community at Qumran* (Leiden: Brill, 2004), 153.

[133] Jokiranta, "An Experiment on Idem Identity in the Qumran Movement," 315.

with the other biblical Qumran literature. Moreover, in the previous section, it was noted that most of the unique readings resonates with Yaḥad documents. Consequently, the unique readings do resonate with Yaḥad messianic sensibilities. For example, first, the theme of Warrior Messiah is well attested in well attested in CD and 1QM (cf. unique reading of Isa 1:24). Secondly, the idea of messianic teacher is well attested in CD, 4QFl (cf. unique reading of Isa 2:3; 26:8). Thirdly, the idea of the Self-understanding of community as messianic has conceptual affinity with CD, 1QM, 1QHᵃ, 4QFl, and 4QPIsaᵃ (cf. unique readings of Isa 4:2, 11:4, and 61:3). Fourthly, the idea of "Messiah as Son of God" is well attested in CD, 1QSa, 11QMelch, 1QM, 4QPGen. Fifthly, the idea of "Messianic age" has conceptual affinity with CD, 1QSa; 11QMelch, 1QM, and 4QPGen (cf. unique reading of Isa 11:9 and 2:3). Sixthly, the idea of "יחד as Messianic community" is reflected in CD and 1QS (cf. unique readings of Isa 40:5; 50:8). Finally, the idea of Messianic Servant resonates with 1QS, 1QHᵃ, and 4QT (cf. unique readings of Isa 42:1; 49:2; 50:4; 52:14; 61:1; and 62:11). It is clear then that the Scroll's messianic ideology resonates with Yaḥad documents.

Finally, it is illustrated that while the Scroll reflects in general Yaḥad Messianism, it is more inclined to the messianic expectation of 1QS community. Therefore, 1QS which is part of Yaḥad documents may be considered as messianic milieu of the Scroll. However, such a view has to be understood in the "network" of messianic ideas of the Qumran literature and the related communities.

Chapter 4

Implications

Any research should not be considered as an end in itself. So do the research in this book. . This book while standing in the line of previous scholarship presents some important implications in relation to textual studies, theological, and sociological implications in the field of Qumran studies.

Implications

Textual Studies

The implications of this book are of great significance to the field of text critical studies in OT as well as Qumran studies. The analysis of the unique readings in chapter 2 and 3 not only shed light on the textual relationships but also conceptual relationships between the texts. Two important observations are to be noted here. First, Qumran exegetes depended on biblical texts in composing non-biblical texts such as CD, 1QS[a, b], 1QM, and 1QH *et al.* For instance, the explicit citations of Isaiah in the non-biblical texts are indicative of Qumran community's experience and reality which was shaped by biblical texts.[1] Secondly, literary and conceptual allusions reflect scribes' theological and ideological motifs behind the changes. Brooke rightly comments that "Qumran commentators atomized the text, fitting it into the new historical context of their own experiences, regardless of its contextual meaning; they selected variant readings to suit their own purposes, occasionally allegorized, and read everything eschatologically, often with the imminent coming of the Messiah in mind."[2] This means that for the Qumran scribe the text is not fixed but it is susceptible to change that would reflect the community's experience, reality and ideology. Michael Fishbane noted that the biblical MSS at Qumran are interpretative in nature and the scribe while copying improved the text.[3]

Likewise, the biblical MSS[4] found at Qumran shows diversity of textual traditions and also varied distinct textual types. For instance, Cross notes that the text of Isaiah found

---

[1] J. J. M Roberts and James H. Charlesworth, "The Importance of Isaiah at Qumran," in *The Bible and the Dead Sea Scrolls*, vol. 1, Princeton Symposium on Judaism and Christian Origins (Waco, Tex: Baylor Univ Pr, 2006), 275.

[2] Brooke, "Biblical Interpretation at Qumran," 1:291.

[3] Michael A Fishbane, "Usè, Authority and Interpretation of Mikra at Qumran," in *Mikra: Text, Translation, Reading and Interpretation of the Hebrew Bible in Ancient Judaism and Early Christianity* (Assen/Maastricht, Netherlands: Fortress, 1988), 367–68.

[4] The word "biblical" is anachronistic here. The reason is that at Qumran there is no fixed or standardized Canon. So, what is meant by "biblical" here is that there are Scrolls found at Qumran which are related to the books in the Hebrew Bible which has been canonized, see, James C VanderKam, *An Introduction to Early Judaism* (Grand Rapids: Eerdmans, 2001), 151.

at Qumran is a witness to the proto-*Masoretic* tradition.[5] In addition to this, other MSS are indicative of diversity and development of textual family in Palestine in the last two centuries of Second Temple Period.[6] For example, the text of Isaiah found at Qumran is an important witness to the Proto-Masoretic tradition.[7] Cross based on the textual evidences found at Qumran regarding biblical MSS identified three geographical locations for the Hebrew textual families *viz.*, Palestinian, Egyptian, and Babylonian.[8] These textual families are represented by a tripartite division of the text types such as MT, LXX, and Sam. Pent. However, Tov based on the emerging textual evidences from Qumran suggests that the textual variety at Qumran does not support the above tripartite division of the texts anymore.[9] In that the emerging evidences are indicative of variety and plurality of texts. Nevertheless whether one can categorize these texts into three neat categories or resort to see the texts in the plurality and variety of texts at Qumran, one must understand that the biblical Scrolls at Qumran provides immense information

---

[5] Frank Moore Cross, "The Contribution of the Qumran Discoveries to the Study of the Biblical Texts," in *Qumran and the History of the Biblical Text* (eds. Frank Moore Cross and Shemaryahu Talmon; Cambridge, Mass: Harvard Univ Pr, 1975), 279.

[6] Cross, "The Contribution of the Qumran Discoveries to the Study of the Biblical Texts," 279.

[7] Cross, "The Contribution of the Qumran Discoveries to the Study of the Biblical Texts," 279.

[8] Cross, "The Contribution of the Qumran Discoveries to the Study of the Biblical Texts," 283.

[9] Emanuel Tov, "A Modern Textual Outlook on the Qumran Scrolls," *HUCA* 53 (1982): 13.

about how the words of the Hebrew Bible were understood at Qumran. This means textual studies as this current research has great lexical significance as well.

The Scroll is a witness of Qumran scribal practice. Talmon rightly noted that if one could read the Scroll without the MT aids such as vowels, text divisions, and syntactical symbols, then new interpretations may be arrived which may reflect original scribal intention.[10] Pulikottil, conversely, indicates that the scribal aspects such as paragraph divisions which constitutes extra spaces and demarcation of major unites by incomplete lines are suggestive of interpretative character of the Scroll.[11] In another instance, number of marginal notations in the Scroll may be indicative of text-divisions. This textual phenomenon is similar to that of 1QS. E. Ulrich notes that such scribal activity indicates that the same scribe who corrected the Scroll wrote the text of 1QS including 1QSᵃ, ᵇ and 4QSamᶜ.[12] Pulikottil understands that such scribal corrections are of great importance as they shed light on "scribal conflicts and concerns" in the Scroll.[13] In addition to this, from an orthographical point of view, the Scroll reflects

---

[10] Talmon, "DSIa as a Witness to Ancient Exegesis of the Book of Isaiah," (ed. Cross and Talmon), 119.

[11] Pulikottil, *Transmission of Biblical Texts*, 16.

[12] Eugene Charles Ulrich, "4QSamᶜ: A Fragmentary Manuscript of 2 Samuel 14-15 from the Scribe of the Serek Hay-Yachad (1QS)," *BASOR* 235 (1979): 1–25.

[13] This strengthens the current research's argument that even the messianic ideology of the Scroll, though distinct may be, resonates with that of 1QS which is part of Yaḥad community, see, Pulikottil, *Transmission of Biblical Texts*, 17.

Qumran texts. The Scroll reflects more *plene* form, though there are variations is the usage between *plene* form and shorter forms. The usage of *plene* form is the "hallmark" of scribal tradition at Qumran.[14] Moreover, such orthographic style is reflected in other Qumran texts such as 1QS, *Pesharim*, 11QT, 1QM, 4QFl, 1QDeut[a], 2QJer, 4QDeut[k], 4QSam[c], 4QIsa[c] etc.[15] Therefore, study of the Scroll has important implications in the area of QSP.

Theological Implications

The messianic ideas of the Scroll revealed different trajectories to be pursued further. First, the self-understanding of the community as messianic had to do with the community's central focus on the *Torah,* holiness, and purity. As already noted, the community's self-understanding as the "Temple of Men" constitutes the above ideas. In fact, such ideological boundaries give a sense of identity.[16] Secondly, the messianic ideals are appropriated in the community life. For instance, as the "interim" community the Yaḥad community claims that they are "doers of Torah."[17] In doing so, they appropriated the ideals of *Torah* in their community life. As a closely knit community there were to eat, pray, deliberate together (1QS 6:2-3), seek God together (1QS 1:1-2), love one another (1QS 1:11), and study *Torah* to atone the land (1QS 8:6, 10). As a result, the community can truly be idealized as "true Israel"

---

[14] Brooke, "Biblical Interpretation at Qumran," 1:302.

[15] Pulikottil, *Transmission of Biblical Texts,* 19.

[16] Schofield, *From Qumran to the Yaḥad,* 278.

[17] Pulikottil, *Transmission of Biblical Texts,* 174.

living in and preparing for the advent of Messiah/s at the end of days. Thirdly, the present study calls for similar research that would illuminate different theological understandings of the Scroll. The same can be applied to other biblical Scrolls at Qumran. In doing so, the "conceptual gap" may be filled in understanding the theological development of various ideas of Second Temple Period and the reflection of the same in the NT.

Sociological Implications

The present study followed a method where the unique readings are analyzed for distinct messianic ideologies that may resonate with Yaḥad community. In that the research focused not only on the messianic idea of the Scroll but also its milieu. Thus, this research provides a "road map" for further research in which different ideologies and the corresponding milieus may be identified. As already noted, Pulikottil after analysing the unique readings from the Scroll proposed that the Scroll may have been copied by a Scribe from Yaḥad community. He arrived at this conclusion by looking at Yaḥad sensibilities in the Scroll. Similarly, Paul Swarup made a thematic study in which he looked at the themes of "eternal planting" and "house of holiness" and indicated how such themes represent self-understanding of the community of the DSS. While Pulikottil focused on the biblical Scroll of Isaiah, Swarup focused on the non-biblical Scrolls. On the other hand, Jokiranta understands various metaphors in the DSS as "identity markers" which are not frozen in time, not to be isolated from their textual worlds, to be understood in the "network of identities."[18] The "network of identities" is indicative of two different types of identities—*Idem* and *Ipse* identity.[19] The former is a "constructed or given" which forms a social identity of the community. The later is self-perception of the community which is created. Consequently, metaphors (themes, ideas, and beliefs) in the texts reflect both *Idem* and *Ipse* identities. So, a text critic must dexterously decipher such metaphors to understand the social identity and the self-perception of the DSS community.

Conclusion

The above discussion outlined the implications of the present study. The present study has significant implication in the area of textual studies, theological understanding of the DSS community, and sociological implications. This book throws light not only on the textual relationships but also conceptual relationships. Furthermore, it was noted that the Scroll is a witness for Qumran scribal practice. The new textual evidence at Qumran is indicative of different textual traditions and plurality of textual types as against stereotyped categorization of three types—MT, LXX, and Sam Pent. In addition to this, the structure of the text and orthography resonates with Yaḥad documents. Theological implications constitute self-understanding of the community as messianic in relation to other theological ideas such as *Torah*, holiness,

---

[18] Jokiranta, "An Experiment on Idem Identity in the Qumran Movement," 315.

[19] Ricoeur pointed out to the distinction between *Idem* and *Ipse* identities, see, Paul Ricoeur reading, *Oneself as Another* (Univ of Chicago Pr, 1992).

and purity. This will help to fill the "conceptual gaps" in our understanding of DSS. Finally, the research has sociological implications as there might be significant ideological and sociological readings in the biblical Scrolls. A further study into this aspect would illumine us to a more enhanced understanding of sociological and ideological milieu of the Scrolls. Such studies would call for as Pulikottil envisioned for text-critical approaches which are to be "expanded and modified" to have a comprehensive understanding of ancient scribal practices and on the usage of biblical Scrolls.[20]

---

[20] Pulikottil, *Transmission of Biblical Texts*, 214–15.

Conclusion

The findings of the Scroll are as follows. The research in this book started with a hypothesis that the variations between the Scroll and the MT are due to scribal modifications which may be intentional or unintentional. Keeping this in mind, the author aimed at investigating the select unique readings for distinct messianic ideas of the Scroll and the corresponding messianic milieu which may be Yaḥad community. The author employed textual criticism in order to first, establish that the select unique readings reflect messianic ideas of the Scroll. Secondly, by using harmonization method, a part of textual criticism, the author aimed to establish that the distinct messianic ideas of the Scroll resonate with Yaḥad Messianism as there might be textual and conceptual affinities.

In Chapter 2 that the select unique readings were analyzed to establish that the select unique readings has messianic significance. The distinct messianic ideas of the Scroll and the corresponding unique readings are as follows. First, the idea of Messiah as Warrior was reflected by Isa 1:24 and 10:24. Secondly, the idea of Messianic teacher at the end of days is reflected by the unique readings 2:3 and 26:8. Thirdly, the self-understanding of community as messianic is reflected by unique readings 4:2, 11:4, and 61:3. Fourthly, the idea of Messiah as the Son of God reflected by unique readings 7:14 and 9:5-6. Fifthly, the idea of Messianic age is reflected by unique reading 11:9. Sixthly, the idea of דחי as Messianic community resonated in the unique readings 40:5 and 50:8. Finally, the idea of Messianic servant is echoed in the unique readings 42:1; 49:2, 6; 50:4; 52:14; 61:1 and 62:11.

In Chapter 3 it was verified that these unique readings resonate with other biblical and Qumran literature. The research in this book found that Yaḥad to be Messianic milieu of the Scroll especially 1QS. This chapter made use of Harmonization method to establish textual and ideological affinities. It was already noted that there need not be always textual affinity but may also be conceptual affinity. So, keeping this in mind, the research identified that the distinct messianic ideas of the Scroll does resonate with other biblical and Qumran literature. First, the idea of "Warrior Messiah" resonates with CD 2:12; 5:21-6:1; 7:18-21 (cf. Num 24:17); 1QM 5:1-2; 11:6-7; 12:9b-15 (cf. Ps 105:15). Secondly, the idea of "Messianic Teacher at the end of days" is reflected by CD 6:7-11 (cf. Isa 26:8); 7:19-20; 20:1; 4QFlor 1:11-13. Thirdly, the "self-understanding of community as messianic" is echoed in CD 2:11-12; 12:21-22; 1QHa 14:14b-15; 16:15b-11; 16:10-11 (cf. Isa 11:1; 14:19; 60:2); 4QFl 3:10-11 (cf. 2 Sam 7:13b-14a); 4QFlor 3:19 (cf. Ps 2:2); and 4QPIsaᵃ 3:17-21a (cf. Isa 11:1-4). Fourthly, the idea of "Messiah as the Son of God" is reflected in 1QSa 2:11-12 (cf. Ps 2:7; Deut 32:1-43) and also this idea reflected in general in 11QMel and 1QM.

Fifthly, the idea of "Messianic Age" is resonated in CD 4:4; 6:11; 7:20; 4Q161 3:17; and 4QFlor 1:11. Sixthly, דחי as Messianic community is reflected in CD 12:22-23; 14:18-19; 19:34-20:1; 1QS 5:6-7; 8:1-16a; 9:3-11; and 10-11. Finally the idea of "Messianic servant" is echoed in CD 6:11 (cf. Deut 18:18 and Hos 10:12); 1QHa 15:10; 15:6-7; 23:14 (cf. Deut 18:18-19; 4QT 5-8; 1QS 9); 4Q521 ii:2, 12 (cf. Ps 146:6-8); and 11QMel 2:15-16.

Based on the above textual and conceptual affinities, it is found that the distinct messianic ideas of the Scroll resonate with Qumran literature in particular with Yaḥad documents. Furthermore, based on the close affinity with 1QS in terms of scribal activity and ideological affinities, it was found that the Messianism of the Scroll is more inclined towards 1QS. However, it was also noted such a view should be understood in the light of different biblical traditions reflected in the Qumran literature.

In Chapter 4, the implications of the study in relation to textual studies, theological, and sociological implications is highlighted. The book provides a road map for further research in deciphering the development of Hebrew language and also understanding ancient scribal practices. This will help to understand the theological and ideological notions behind scribal variants so that the "conceptual gaps" may be filled in understanding the context, society, and political dimensions of Qumran community. Such an endeavor calls for a different way of using textual criticism in which the aim need not always be to adjudicate the text for a better reading but deciphering scribal intentions of the variants. The present study is an example of such an attempt in which the distinct messianic ideas of the Scroll were identified and located its messianic milieu i.e., Yaḥad in particular 1QS.

As indicated earlier that similar type of studies may be pursued in which various theological and ideological motifs of the scribe can be identified. This will help to have comprehensive understanding of the theological and ideological development during Second Temple Period. Furthermore, such studies would help to fill the "conceptual gaps" in the New Testament studies. The present study focused on one theological theme of "Messiah." Further research may be done focusing on different theological themes of the other biblical scrolls. Moreover, textual study as this book employed may also be applied to understand the development and the uniqueness of the Hebrew language as reflected by the unique readings. In other words, a research on the Hebrew grammar of the Scroll may be pursued. Conversely, the research can be furthered to see whether Hebrew grammar as reflected by unique readings resonate with Yaḥad Hebrew grammar. Such an endeavor would be of great significance in terms of syntactical, lexical, orthographic, paleographic, and development of Hebrew language during Second Temple Period.

Bibliography

Allegro, J. M. "Further Messianic References in Qumran Literature." *Journal of Biblical Literature.* 75.3 (1956): 174–87.

Allegro, John M, ed. *Discoveries in the Judean Desert of Jordan, v 5: Qumrân Cave 4.* Oxford: Clarendon Pr, 1968.

Baker, David W. "Further Examples of the Wāw Explicativum." *Vetus Testamentum.* 30.2 (1980): 129–36.

Barthélemy, Dominique, and Jozef Tadeusz Milik. *Discoveries in the Judean Desert, v 1: Qumran Cave 1.* Oxford: Clarendon, 1955.

Bautch, Kelley Coblentz. "Textual Criticism Apocrypha and Deuterocanonical Books." Edited by Steven L McKenzie. *The Oxford Encyclopedia of Biblical Interpretation.* Oxford: Oxford Univ Pr, 2013.

Black, M. "Theological Conceptions in the Dead Sea Scrolls." *Exegetisk Arsbok* 18–19 (1953): 72–97.

Blenkinsopp, Joseph. *Isaiah 1-39 A New Translation with Introduction and Commentary.* Edited by William Foxwell Albright and David Noel Freedman. Vol. 19. The Anchor Bible. NY: Doubleday, 2000.

————. *Isaiah 40-55 A New Translation with Introduction and Commentary.* Edited by William Foxwell Albright and David Noel Freedman. Vol. 19A. The Anchor Bible. NY: Doubleday, 2002.

Brooke, George J. "Biblical Interpretation at Qumran." Pages 287–319 in *The Bible and the Dead Sea Scrolls The Princeton Symposium on the Dead Sea Scrolls.* Edited by James H. Charlesworth. Vol. 1. Scripture and the Scrolls. Waco, TX: Baylor University Press, 2006.

Brooke, George J. *Exegesis at Qumran: 4QFlorilegium in Its Jewish Context.* Journal for the Study of the Old Testament: Supplement Series29. Sheffield: JSOT Pr, 1985.

Brown, Raymond Edward. "Messianism of QumrâN." *Catholic Biblical Quarterly.* 19.1 (1957): 53–82.

________. *The Birth of the Messiah: A Commentary on the Infancy Narratives in the Gospels of Matthew and Luke.* Anchor Bible reference library. New York: Doubleday; Geoffrey Chapman, 1993.

Brownlee, W. H. *The Meaning of the Qumran Scrolls for the Bible: With Special Attention to the Book of Isaiah.* NY: Oxford university press, 1964.

________. "The Servant of the LORD in the Qumran Scrolls I." *Bulletin of the American Schools of Oriental Research* 132 (1953): 8–15.

Bruce, F. F. *Biblical Exegesis in the Qumran Texts.* London: The Tyndale Press, 1960.

Burrows, Millar. "Orthography, Morphology, and Syntax of the St Mark's Isaiah Manuscript." *Journal of Biblical Literature.* 68.3 (1949): 195–211.

________. "The Newly Discovered Jerusalem Scrolls II the Contents and Significance of the Manuscripts." *Biblical Archaeology.* 11.3 (1948): 57–61.

Chamberlain, John V. "Functions of God as Messianic Titles in the Complete Qumran Isaiah Scroll." *Vetus Testamentum.* 5.4 (1955): 366–72.

Charlesworth, James H. "Community Organization." Edited by Lawrence H Schiffman and James C VanderKam. *Encyclopedia of the Dead Sea Scroll.* NY: Oxford Univ Pr, 2000.

Clements, R. E. *Isaiah 1-39.* Edited by R. E. Clements and Matthew Black. The New Century Bible Commentary. Grand Rapids, MI: Wm. B. Eerdmans Publishing, 1980.

Clines, David J. A., ed. *The Dictionary of Classical Hebrew V.* Sheffield: Sheffield Phoenix Press, 2011.

________, ed. *The Dictionary of Classical Hebrew VIII* ש־ת. Sheffield: Sheffield Phoenix Press, 2011.

________, ed. "מַטֶּה." *Dictionary of Classical Hebrew.* Sheffield: Sheffield Academic Pr, 2001.

Collins, John J. *The Scepter and the Star Messianism in the Light of the Dead Sea Scrolls.* 2nd ed. Grand Rapids, MI: Eerdmans, 2010.

Collins, John J. (John Joseph). "Beyond the Qumran Community: Social Organization in the Dead Sea Scrolls." *Dead Sea Discoveries.* 16.3 (2009): 351–69.

Cross, Frank Moore. "Qumran Cave I." *Journal of Biblical Literature.* 75.2 (1956): 121–25.

————. "The Contribution of the Qumran Discoveries to the Study of the Biblical Texts." Pages 278–92 in *Qumran and the History of the Biblical Text.* Edited by Frank Moore Cross and Shemaryahu Talmon. Cambridge, Mass: Harvard Univ Pr, 1975.

Crowe, Brandon D. "The Song of Moses and Divine Begetting in Matt 1,20." *Biblica* 90.1 (2009): 47–58.

Davies, Philip R. "Eschatology at Qumran." *Journal of Biblical Literature.* 104.1 (1985): 39–55.

————. *The Damascus Covenant: An Interpretation of the "Damascus Document."* JSOT Pr, 1982.

Dupont-Sommer, André. *The Essene Writings from Qumran.* Meridian Books. Cleveland: World Pub, 1962.

Eissfeldt, Otto. "Promises of Grace to David in Isaiah 55:1-5." Pages 196–207 in *Israel's Prophetic Heritage; Essays in Honor of James Muilenburg.* Harper, 1962.

Fishbane, Michael A. "Use, Authority and Interpretation of Mikra at Qumran." Pages 339–77 in *Mikra: Text, Translation, Reading and Interpretation of the Hebrew Bible in Ancient Judaism and Early Christianity.* Assen/Maastricht, Netherlands: Fortress, 1988.

Fitzmyer, Joseph A. *The Dead Sea Scrolls and the Christian Origins.* Studies in the Dead Sea Scrolls and Related Literature. Grand Rapids, MI; Cambridge, UK: William B. Eerdmans Publishing Company, 2000.

García Martínez, Florentino. "Two Messianic Figures in the Qumran Texts." Pages 14–40 in *Current Research and Technological Developments on the Dead Sea Scrolls: Conference on the Texts from the Judean Desert, Jerusalem, 30 April 1995.* Leiden: E J Brill, 1996.

Gesenius' Hebrew Grammar. Edited by E. Kautzsch. Translated by A. E. Cowley. 2d ed. Oxford, 1910.

Goldingay, John, and David Payne. *Isaiah 40-55*. Vol. 1. The International Critical Commentary. NY: T. & T. Clark International, 2006.

______. *Isaiah 40-55*. Vol. II. The International Critical Commentary. NY: T. & T. Clark International, 2006.

Gordis, Robert. "'Begotten' Messiah in the Qumran Scrolls." *Vetus Testamentum*. 7.2 (1957): 191–94.

Gordon, Robert P. "Transmission of Biblical Texts in Qumran: The Case of the Large Isaiah Scroll 1QIsaa." *Journal for the Study of the Old Testament*. 26.5 (2002): 224–224.

Hendel, Ronald S. "Assessing the Text-Critical Theories of the Hebrew Bible after Qumran." Pages 281–302 in *The Oxford Handbook of the Dead Sea Scrolls*. Edited by John J. Collins and Timothy H. Lim. Oxford handbooks in religion and theology. Oxford: Oxford Univ Pr, 2010.

Hoegenhaven, Jesper. "The First Isaiah Scroll from Qumran (1QIsa) and the Massoretic Text: Some Reflections with Special Regard to Isaiah 1-12." *Journal for the Study of the Old Testament*. 28 (1984): 17–35.

Horgan, Maurya P. *Pesharim: Qumran Interpretations of Biblical Books*. Catholic Biblical Quarterly. Catholic Biblical Assoc, 1979.

Jermias, J. "Ηλ(ε)Ιας." Edited by Gerhard Kittel. Theological Dictionary of the New Testament. vol. II. Grand Rapids, MI: Eerdmans, 1964.

Jokiranta, Jutta. "An Experiment on Idem Identity in the Qumran Movement." *Dead Sea Discoveries*. 16.3 (2009): 309–29.

Kaiser, Otto. *Isaiah 1-12 A Commentary*. Edited by Peter Ackroyd, James Barr, Bernhard W Anderson, and John Bright. Translated by John Bowden. Second. The Old Testament Library. Philadelphia: The Westminster Press, 1983.

______. *Isaiah 13-39 A Commentary*. Edited by G. Ernest Wright, John Bright, James Barr, and Peter Ackroyd. Translated by R. A. Wilson. Second. The Old Testament Library. Philadelphia: The Westminster Press, 1973.

Knibb, Michael A. "The Teacher of Righteousness - a Messianic Title." Pages 51–65 in *A Tribute to Geza Vermes: Essays on Jewish and Christian Literature and History*. Sheffield, Eng: JSOT Pr, 1990.

Kooij, Arie van der. *Die Alten Textzeugen Des Jesajabuches*. Fribourg, Switzerland: Universitätsverlag; Vandenhoeck & Ruprecht, 1981.

Kuhn, Karl G. "The Two Messiahs of Aaron and Israel." Page 54 in *The Scrolls and the New Testament*. New York: Crossroad, 1992.

Kutscher, Edward Yechezkel. *The Language and Linguistic Background of the Isaiah Scroll: I QIsa*. Leiden: Brill, 1974.

La Sor, William Sanford. "'Messiahs of Aaron and Israel.'" *Vetus Testamentum*. 6.4 (1956): 425–29.

Laurin, Robert B. "Problem of Two Messiahs in the Qumran Scrolls." *Rev. Qumran* 4.1 (1963): 39–52.

Liver, Jacob. "The Doctrine of the Two Messiahs in Sectarian Literature in the Time of the Second Commonwealth." *Harvard Theological Review*. 52.3 (1959): 149–86.

Newsom, Carol A. *The Self as Symbolic Space: Constructing Identity and Community at Qumran*. Leiden: Brill, 2004.

Novakovic, Lidija. *Messiah, the Healer of the Sick: A Study of Jesus as the Son of David in the Gospel of Matthew*. Wissenschaftliche Untersuchungen zum Neuen Testament. Tübingen: Mohr Siebeck, 2003.

Orlinsky, Harry Meyer. "Studies in the St Mark's Isaiah Scroll, Pt 6." *Hebrew Union College Annual*. 25 (1954): 85–92.

Parry, Donald W., and Elisha Qimron, eds. *The Great Isaiah Scroll (1QIsaa)*. Vol. XXXII. New Studies on the Texts of the Desert of Judah. Leiden: Brill, 1999.

Puech, Émile. "Fragments d'un Apocryphe de Lévi et Le Personnage Eschatologique: 4QTestLévic-d(?) Et 4QAJa." Pages 449–501 in *The Madrid Qumran Congress: Proceedings of the International Congress on the Dead Sea Scrolls, Madrid, 18-21 March 1991*. Leiden: E J Brill, 1992.

Pulikottil, Paulson. *Transmission of Biblical Texts in Qumran The Case of the Large Isaiah Scroll 1QISaa*. Edited by Lester L. Grabbe and James H. Charlesworth. Journal for the Study of the Pseudepigrapha Supplement Series 34. England: Sheffield Academic Press, 2001.

Rad, Gerhard von. *Old Testament Theology; v 2; Tr by D M G Stalker*. New York: Harper and Row, 1966.

Reider, J. "On MSHTY Int He Qumran Scrolls." *Bulletin of the American Schools of Oriental Research*. 134 (1954): 27–28.

Ricoeur, Paul. *Oneself as Another*. Univ of Chicago Pr, 1992.

Roberts, J. J. M, and James H. Charlesworth. "The Importance of Isaiah at Qumran." Pages 273–86 in *The Bible and the Dead Sea Scrolls*. Vol. 1. Princeton Symposium on Judaism and Christian Origins. Waco, Tex: Baylor Univ Pr, 2006.

Rosenbloom, Joseph R. *The Dead Sea Isaiah Scroll: A Literary Analysis: A Comparison with the Masoretic Text and the Biblia Hebraica*. Eerdmans, 1970.

Rubinstein, Arie. "Notes on the Use of the Tenses in the Variant Readings of the Isaiah Scroll." *Vetus Testam.* 3.1 (1953): 92–95.

———. "The Theological Aspect of Some Variant Readings in the Isaiah Scroll." *Journal of Jewish Studies.* 6.4 (1955): 187–200.

Samuel Raj, J. R. *The "Anointed Ones" in the Qumran Literature*. Delhi: ISPCK, 2005.

Schniedewind, William M. "Qumran Hebrew as an Antilanguage." *J. Biblic. Lit.* 118.2 (1999): 235–52.

Schofield, Alison. *From Qumran to the Yaḥad: A New Paradigm of Textual Development for The Community Rule*. Studies on the texts of the desert of Judah. Leiden: Brill, 2009.

Skehan, Patrick William. "The Qumran Manuscripts and the Textual Criticism." Pages 212–22 in *Qumran and the History of the Biblical Text*. Edited by Frank Moore Cross and Shemaryahu Talmon. Cambridge, Massachusetts: Harvard University Press, 1978.

Starcky, Jean. "Les Quatre Étapes Du Messianisme à Qumran." *Revue Biblique* 70.4 (1963): 481–505.

Stuhlman, Daniel D. "A Variant Text from the Isaiah Scroll." *Jewish Bible Quaterly.* 25.3 (1997): 177–84.

Swarup, Paul. *The Self-Understanding of the Dead Sea Scrolls Community: An Eternal Planting, a House of Holiness*. Library of Second Temple studies. London: T&T Clark, 2006.

Talmon, Shemaryahu. "DSIa as a Witness to Ancient Exegesis of the Book of Isaiah." Pages 116–26 in *Qumran and the History of the Biblical Text*. Edited by Frank Moore Cross and Shemaryahu Talmon. Cambridge, Massachusetts: Harvard University Press, 1978.

———. "DSIa as a Witness to Ancient Exegesis of the Book of Isaiah." Pages 116–26 in *Qumran and the History of the Biblical Text*. Edited by Frank Moore Cross and Shemaryahu Talmon. Cambridge, Mass: Harvard Univ Pr, 1975.

————. "The Concept of Māšîah and Messianism in Early Judaism." Pages 79–115 in *The Messiah: Developments in Earliest Judaism and Christianity*. Minneapolis: Fortress Pr, 1992.

————. "The Internal Diversification of Judaism in the Early Second Temple Period." Pages 16–43 in *Jewish Civilization in the Hellenistic-Roman Period*. Sheffield, England: JSOT Pr, 1991.

————. "Waiting for the Messiah at Qumran." Pages 111–37 in *Judaisms and Their Messiahs at the Turn of the Christian Era*. Edited by Jacob Neusner, W. S. Green, and E. S. Frerichs. Cambridge, England: Cambridge Univ Pr, 1987.

Tov, Emanuel. *Hebrew Bible, Greek Bible and Qumran: Collected Essays*. Mohr Siebeck, 2008.

————. *Textual Criticism of the Hebrew Bible*. Third. Minneapolis: Fortress Press, 2012.

————. "The Nature and Backgrounds of Harmonizations in Biblical Manuscripts." *Journal for Study of the Old Testament*. 10.31 (1985): 3–29.

Ulrich, Eugene Charles. "4QSam[a]: A Fragmentary Manuscript of 2 Samuel 14-15 from the Scribe of the Serek Hay-Yachad (1QS)." *Bulletin of the American Schools of Oriental Research*. 235 (1979): 1–25.

VanderKam, James C. *An Introduction to Early Judaism*. Grand Rapids: Eerdmans, 2001.

Vanderkam, James, and Peter Flint. *The Meaning of the Dead Sea Scrolls*. NY: HarperSan Francisco, 2002.

Vermes, Geza. *The Complete Dead Sea Scrolls in English*. Rev. England: Penguin books, 2004.

Vermès, Géza. "The Oxford Forum for Qumran Research: Seminar on the Rule of War from Cave 4 (4Q285)." *Journal of Jewish Studies*. 43.1 (1992): 85–94.

Waltke, Bruce K., and M. O'Connor. *An Introduction to Biblical Hebrew Syntax*. Winona Lake, Indiana: 1990.

Watson, Wilfred G. E. *Classical Hebrew Poetry A Guide to Its Techniques*. Journal for the Study of the Old Testament: Supplement Series 26. Sheffield: JSOT Pr, 1986.

Watts, John D. W. *Isaiah 1-33*. Edited by David A Hubbard and Glenn W Barker. Vol. 24. Word Biblical Commentary. Waco, TX: Word Books, Publisher, 1985.

———. *Isaiah 34-66*. Edited by Bruce M. Metzer, David A Hubbard, and Glenn W Barker. Vol. 25. Word Biblical Commentary. Waco, TX: Word Books, Publisher, 1987.

Westermann, Claus. *Isaiah 40-66 A Commentary*. Translated by David. M. G. Stalker. The Old Testament Library. Philadelphia: The Westminster Press, 1969.

Wildberger, Hans. *Isaiah 1-12 A Commentary*. Translated by Thomas Trapp. Vol. 24. A Continental Commentary. Minneapolis: Augsburg Fortress, 1991.

Williamson, H G M. "Transmission of Biblical Texts in Qumran: The Case of the Large Isaiah Scroll 1QIsaa." *Journal of Theological Studies*. 54.2 (2003): 641–46.

Williamson, Hugh. *Isaiah 1-5 (ICC): A Critical and Exegetical Commentary*. The International Critical Commentary. NY: A&C Black, 2006.

Wise, Michael O. "4QFlorilegium and the Temple of Adam." *Revue de Qumran* 15.1–2 (1991): 103–32.

———. *The First Messiah*. San Francisco: HarperSan Francisco, 1999.

———. "The Temple Scroll and the Teacher of Righteousness." Pages 121–47 in *Mogilany 1989: Papers on the Dead Sea Scrolls Offered in Memory of Jean Carmignac*. Cracow: Enigma Pr, 1993.

Würthwein, Ernst. *The Text of the Old Testament An Introduction to the Biblica Heraica*. Translated by Erroll F. Rhodes. Second. Grand Rapids, MI: William B. Eerdmans Publishing Company, 1995.

Wyngaarden, Martin Jacob. "The Servant of Jehovah in Isaiah and the Dead Sea Scrolls." *Bulletin of Evangelical Theological Society*. 1.3 (1958): 20–24.

Index